Leading Schools with
Unique Populations

Leading Schools with Unique Populations

An International Perspective on School Leadership

Edited by Peter R. Litchka

ROWMAN & LITTLEFIELD
Lanham • Boulder • New York • London

Published by Rowman & Littlefield
A wholly owned subsidiary of The Rowman & Littlefield Publishing Group, Inc.
4501 Forbes Boulevard, Suite 200, Lanham, Maryland 20706
www.rowman.com

6 Tinworth Street, London SE11 5AL, United Kingdom

Copyright © 2019 by Peter R. Litchka

All rights reserved. No part of this book may be reproduced in any form or by any electronic or mechanical means, including information storage and retrieval systems, without written permission from the publisher, except by a reviewer who may quote passages in a review.

British Library Cataloguing in Publication Information Available

Library of Congress Cataloging-in-Publication Data Available

Library of Congress Control Number: 2019950155

ISBN 978-1-4758-5290-5 (cloth : alk. paper)
ISBN 978-1-4758-5291-2 (paper : alk. paper)
ISBN 978-1-4758-5292-9 (electronic)

To Mike, Paul, and Ron:
*Friends for more than fifty years—
and, I hope, for many more! LaSalle '68.*

Contents

Foreword		ix
Acknowledgments		xv
Introduction		xvii
Chapter 1	Beating the Odds: Transforming At-Risk Schools to Sources of Hope and Inspiration *Adam E. Nir*	1
Chapter 2	School Leadership to Increase Inclusive Education Practices in China, Thailand, and Turkey *Tanyathorn Hauwadhanasuk, Min Zhuang, Susan Toft Everson, Shenggang Yu, and Mustafa Karnas*	17
Chapter 3	Educational Leadership in Latin America: Equipping Orphans and Vulnerable Children for Success Beyond the Institution *Calvin G. Roso*	37
Chapter 4	Notre Dame Mission Volunteers–AmeriCorps—A National Program with Significant Local Impact *Peter R. Litchka*	55
About the Authors		77
About the Editor		79

Foreword

This book edited by Peter R. Litchka provides fascinating insights into the lived experiences of learners who possess very special needs and the outstanding teachers and administrators who work for them to provide them with their right to education in their respective societies. The book specifically focuses on children with exceptionalities, who are often the most vulnerable children, in seven distinct national contexts: China, Colombia, Guatemala, Israel, Thailand, Turkey, and the United States.

The four chapters are presented by eight researchers who have studied children who need special care and attention because of circumstances that contributed to them being significantly different from many of their peers in academic achievement, home experiences, physical attributes, and/or psychological dispositions.

Yet, these children are all aspiring learners who want the opportunities to be educated for personal as well as career and altruistic purposes. They want to play an active part in their respective contexts, and they know that education points the way. As W. E. B. Du Bois said more than a century ago, "Education is the great lever that lifts society members and enables them to become contributing members of their society."

These chapters contain stories of the school leaders from around the world who went beyond the normal expectations in their educational settings to address the challenges associated with teaching these children and had the commitment to educate them in intensively creative and caring ways. There is no doubt that most, if not all, contemporary educators truly believe, as

George Evans said, that "every student can learn, just not on the same day, or the same way"; however, how to help them learn in a consistent and well-coordinated manner is not often articulated. The chapters of this book provide valuable insights that both experienced and aspiring educational leaders can use to address the special needs of these various exceptional students.

I have spent over fifty years in public education advocating that educators take more child-centered and less content-centered approaches to teaching and learning. I truly believe that all children can learn, but not in the same way or on the same day, and that all children are truly gifted and talented and that it is our professional responsibility to identify both those special needs of the children we teach to their needs and abilities.

It is imperative that educators devise, with caring diligence, educational programs, strategies, activities, and evaluations based on those identified student needs and strengths. I composed two poems, "Our Quest for Understanding" (Polka, 1996) and "US Educators Refuse Leaving Any Student Behind . . . But" (Polka, 2009) that both reflect my unwavering commitment to individualizing instruction and differentiating learning.

"Our Quest for Understanding" addresses the philosophical approach that should be employed for each of us to appreciate the complex uniqueness of each person in our world as opposed to standardizing human endeavors and experiences. This poem was inspired by the work of constructivist educators and humanist thinkers who promoted the importance of appreciating differences throughout history, such as Quintilian, Comenius, Rousseau, Pestalozzi, Dewey, and Gardner. The essence of the poem was cogently captured by Albert Einstein when in 1929 he stated, "I believe in standardizing automobiles. I do not believe in standardizing human beings. Standardization is a great peril which threatens American culture."

The standardization paradigm, when applied to people, has had deleterious effects on our world, especially over the last century or so, but the contributors to this book, who share their thoughts, ideas, and lived experiences, definitely know that and have dedicated their work to helping those students who do not fit the prototypical school standards and expectations. They have recognized the imperativeness of appreciating differences in teaching and learning.

Our Quest for Understanding
We have searched diligently for
similar
patterns, structures, and realities among
different
people, things, and ideas;
in our quest for simple understanding.

We have planned continuously to
standardize
events, options, and interactions among
different
people, things, and ideas;
in our quest for simple understanding.

We have implemented forcibly, with
precision
programs, models, and approaches among
different
people, things, and ideas;
in our quest for simple understanding.

We must commence seriously to
humanize
relations, histories, and futures among
different
people, things, and ideas;
in our quest for enhanced understanding.

And, we must realize naturally to
appreciate
uniqueness and individuality among
different
people, things, and ideas;
in our quest for genuine understanding.

Walter S. Polka (1996)

Since the end of the twentieth century, educational leaders have also focused on standardizing the learning experiences for students at all levels of the instructional spectrum. There has been an international, intentional, and comprehensive focus on developing curriculum, instructional programs, evaluation strategies, and packaged "teacher-proof" materials that reduce the significance of everyone under the guise of improving the achievement of more students.

The United States has been a policy leader and economic driver in this movement and has influenced this standardized education orientation throughout the world with such packaged learning systems as the Common Core Curriculum. Caring for the individual learning needs of students has been subjugated to national expectations to quantify student achievement on a mass scale. Based on my teaching throughout the United States and listening to the concerns of educators at the dawn of the twenty-first century, I wrote the poem "US Educators Refuse Leaving Any Student Behind . . . But" based on the heartfelt views of so many educators and their incensed reactions to the increased standardization of learning as a matter of government policies.

> **US Educators Refuse Leaving Any Student Behind . . . But**
> US educators refuse leaving any student behind
> vis-à-vis individual development!
> But, we will not promulgate
> standardization
> because each person is unique
> and possesses special gifts and talents.
>
> We refuse leaving any student behind
> involving intellectual development.
> But, we won't restrict
> thinking
> since each person is unique
> and some knowledge is incalculable.
>
> We refuse leaving any student behind
> regarding artistic development.
> But, we won't pre-frame
> expressions
> since each person is unique
> and beauty is in the beholder's eye.

We refuse leaving any student behind
relating to musical development.
But, we won't pre-set
rhythms
since each person is unique
and apt music is in the listener's ear.

We refuse leaving any student behind
concerning physical development.
But, we won't pre-judge
athleticism
because each person is unique
and body prowess takes many forms.

We refuse leaving any student behind
concerning analytical development.
But, we won't pre-figure
problem-solving
since each person is unique
and divergent solutions show creativity.

We refuse leaving any student behind
related to curiosity development.
But, we won't pre-fix
explorations
since each person is unique
and our universe needs more discovery.

We refuse leaving any student behind
regarding patriotic development.
But, we won't subvert
dissent
since each person is unique
and history epitomizes our independence.

We refuse leaving any student behind
involving cultural development.
But, we won't decree
assimilation
since each person is unique
and enriched citizenship is multifaceted.

> US educators, thus, refuse leaving any student behind
> vis-à-vis educational development!
> Yet, we will not abdicate
> individualization
> because each person is unique
> and differences are hallmarks of our society.
>
> Walter S. Polka (2009)

The above poem resonates with the research findings of the authors of the chapters of this book, Adam Nir (Chapter 1); Tanyathorn Hauwadhanasuk, Min Zhuang, Susan Toft Everson, Shenggang Yu, and Mustafa Karnas (Chapter 2); Calvin Roso (Chapter 3); and Peter Litchka (Chapter 4), who have provided examples of why and how caring and creative approaches need to be comprehensively and continuously employed in all educational settings. Their research has given voice to administrators, teachers, and students and reinforced the concepts of both of the above poems.

The lived experiences expressed in this book need to not only be read and heard by educators today but also reflected in current teaching-learning settings. It is an absolute necessity to differentiate instruction in a caring student-centered fashion, especially for those students at most risk because they are not part of the typical majority in contemporary schools.

John Dewey established a key concept for educators to keep in mind when reflecting about children and schools in his 1902 publication, *The Child and the Curriculum*. He suggested that educators should not ask the question, "Is this child ready for this school?" but rather, "Is this school ready for this child?" This book clearly illustrates that schools, teachers, and administrators need to think about schooling as Dewey did over one hundred years ago to develop a mindset with a focus on individual student needs.

We know that the constructivist approaches and strategies identified in this book are key to the development of all children, but they are especially important to the growth and development of children who are considered our most vulnerable students because of circumstances beyond their control.

Walter Polka
March 2019
Niagara University, New York

Acknowledgments

I wish to thank the International Society for Educational Planning (ISEP), of which I have been a member since 2006. ISEP is committed to fostering healthy and pertinent discourse regarding education, and this commitment first and foremost is of a global nature. Without ISEP, I doubt I would have been able to travel to countries such as Cyprus, Hungary, Israel, Poland, and Turkey, but of more importance, I would not have been able to meet educators from these and other countries in a professional and collegial manner. And thank you to Walter Polka, my friend and mentor, who encouraged me to join ISEP back in 2006.

To Loyola University Maryland, particularly Joshua Smith, the dean of the School of Education, thank you for your support, encouragement, and guidance.

I wish to thank Stephanie Dunford for her keen editorial sense and critique in the development of this book. Her insights, questions, critiques, and reviews were most helpful.

And, finally, to the graduate students in the Educational Leadership Program at Loyola University Maryland, who continue to amaze me with their energy, enthusiasm, and quest to make a difference, both as teachers and as aspiring leaders.

Introduction

> Where justice is denied, where poverty is enforced, where ignorance prevails, and where any one class is made to feel that society is an organized conspiracy to oppress, rob, and degrade them, neither persons nor property will be safe.
>
> —Frederick Douglass

This is the second book in a series that examines school leadership from the perspective of practitioners, scholars, and policy makers from around the world. The first book, *School Leadership That Works—Ideas from Around the World* (2019), focused on preparing future school leaders and supporting current school leaders.

Like the first book, this book is also about building bridges among scholars, policy makers, and practitioners within the field of educational leadership throughout the world. Of course, the use of the word *bridge* is clearly symbolic in terms of building relationships based on the principles of listening, collaborating, and reflecting with others, who, for many reasons, may not have had the opportunity to do so. Perhaps walls between us (symbolically or even real) had been built that, based on perceived or authentic differences, prevented such interaction from occurring. Or maybe we just did not have the opportunity to engage with others from around the world.

Over the past decade, I have had the wonderful opportunity to travel to countries such as Canada, Cyprus, Israel, Poland, and Turkey to engage in scholarly activities, including independent research and scholarly presentations. It is this experience, along with being a member of the International Society for Educational Planning, that the foundation of this book and others within the series has been built upon. As technology continues to speed up our lives and, in some cases, make communication and interaction easier—but maybe not better—the hope is that this series of books will offer opportunities to learn more about our colleagues around the world, their cultures, their education systems, and their perceptions of the current context of educational leadership.

Of course, we know that school leadership matters! Countless studies have concluded that the leader of the school—usually the principal or headmaster/mistress—is the most significant factor in determining the overall success of a school and its students. Accordingly, the school leader, through her or his beliefs, attitudes, and actions, creates the overall climate of the school in terms of how teachers teach and how students learn. This is particularly evident and of significance in the administration of programs in a school where there are unique and special students.

This book brings an international perspective of school leadership; it examines how such leadership can have a positive impact on students considered to be "unique." At one time, such students considered "unique" or "special" were often placed in special education programs and/or special schools to address their physical, emotional, and/or mental disabilities. Through legislation and changes in beliefs, many countries have changed approaches with these students from a "warehouse" approach, where such students were placed in special schools, to more of an inclusive approach, where such students remain in their particular home school in an environment that is more inclusive and less restrictive.

Over the past two decades or so, schools around the globe have been experiencing a significant increase in not only the number of "traditional" types of students needing special services but also a new generation of unique and diverse students, including those with

- sexual identity and orientation differences;
- extreme social and economic inequities; or
- cultural differences arising from the significant increase in the number of migrant families fleeing unstable nations and settling into more secure environments that may be totally different in terms of language, religion, and other cultural features.

Through their education systems, many nations are moving from compliance to results and from deficit models to support and prevention; they are becoming more inclusive of unique and special students. Thus, school leaders, if provided the opportunity and support, can have a significant impact on the education of *all* students by linking their leadership to the following tenets:

1. *All* students are accepted at our school.
2. *All* students and *each* student can learn and be successful.
3. *All* teachers can teach *all* students and are responsible for the learning and success of *all* students.
4. The school leader is responsible for the education of *all* students and the professional growth of *each* and *every* teacher in the school.

Obviously, this is a great task to add on to everything else that is expected of the school leader. However, it is evident that schools are where diversity is accepted and honored, and where there will be a much greater change for the success of *all* students.

To begin this book, Adam Nir of Israel presents "Beating the Odds: Transforming At-Risk Schools to Sources of Hope and Inspiration," an examination of the role and leadership abilities of a particular principal in Israel who was faced with a significant number of at-risk students. By using effective leadership behaviors, strategies, and values, he was able to improve the education of *all* at this particular school.

Next, Tanyathorn Hauwadhanasuk, Min Zhuang, Susan Toft Everson, Shenggang Yu, and Mustafa Karnas present three examples of inclusionary practices from schools in China, Thailand, and Turkey and analyze common elements among them and their relationship to effective leadership.

Calvin Roso presents "Educational Leadership in Latin America: Equipping Orphans and Vulnerable Children for Success Beyond the Institution," an examination of how students considered to be extremely vulnerable and marginalized—in this case, orphans—can be successfully educated and the impact school leaders can have on such young people.

The final chapter in this book is by the book's editor, Peter Litchka, who presents a synopsis of three evaluations of the effect that the Notre Dame Mission Volunteers–AmeriCorps program has on the students it serves in mostly urban, high-poverty areas of the United States. This chapter provides a perspective on school leadership not from the principal's office but from an organization devoted to improving the education of marginalized students through various means and resources.

CHAPTER ONE

Beating the Odds

Transforming At-Risk Schools to Sources of Hope and Inspiration

Adam E. Nir

Our world is shifting toward globalization as local and national perspectives become open and exposed to a broader spectrum of ideas, goods, and services originated in other cultural and social settings.

Globalization encourages the movement of people from their country of residence and exposes individuals to interactions with others coming from different cultures and nationalities. Under these newly created circumstances, states find it almost impossible to control their borders in the way they used to, following international agreements whereby control of borders does not operate on a national level anymore. This trend is also intensified as international travel becomes much cheaper and easier. One of the most prominent examples of this global tendency may be evident in the Schengen Area, which allows for free movement among European countries.

Two major incentives foster migration and the tendency of people to leave their homeland and start a new life in some other country of which they are not natives and citizens. The first one is economic: Obtaining higher wages and better-paying jobs is one way to improve individual well-being. Therefore, workers are encouraged to take up employment as migrants or as foreign workers in countries where the pay level is higher. According to the International Labour Organization, as of 2014, there were an estimated 232 million international migrants in the world, of which approximately half were estimated to be employed (International Labour Organization, 2015). The second incentive fostering migration is associated with international violence often leading to humanitarian crises. As I am writing this chapter, millions of people around the globe are forced to abandon their countries and homes and escape for the sake of saving their lives.

The conflict in Syria continues to be by far the largest force for migration, but the ongoing violence in Afghanistan and Iraq, and the abuses taking place in Eritrea, Somalia, and Sudan, are also leading people to look for new lives elsewhere. As a result, 16.1 million people are considered refugees living outside their home countries (UNHCR, 2016).

Hence, while most of us continue with our daily routines, waking up in the morning, sending our children off to school, and going to work, our globalized world creates a growing number of people living in instability and fear, coercing them to look for work elsewhere or to run for their lives and change their status from citizens to refugees.

The growing number of refugees and work migrants seems to undermine globalization that weakens states' capacity to control their borders. Rather, this growing trend seems to strengthen in some paradoxical ways the sense of national consciousness among citizens. Nationalism is enhanced as society's members want their states to better control their borders by limiting the entrance and stay of refugees. Elections around the world, particularly in North America, Europe, and Australia, have been fought, won, and lost on the trepidation about migration.

In practice, refugees and work migrants are becoming a significant phenomenon and concern for governments and societies more than ever before. Although not all of them cross borders legally, their presence in the absorbing states is overriding, and their needs and dependency on various services, such as social, health, and educational services, is similar to the needs of any of the country's citizens. From a social justice perspective, these circumstances create an enormous challenge for governments as any official attempt to provide equal services to refugees or work migrants is most likely to encounter the opposition of citizens who consider this tendency an act at their expense.

Social Justice in Education

The growing number of people migrating from their homelands with the intention of improving their well-being creates a new reality, provoking the debate on social justice. In recent years, *social justice* has become a buzz term and a major concern for politicians, social activists, and scholars.

In essence, a social justice perspective argues for the need to ensure that opportunities and resources are fairly distributed within society and that individuals and groups work toward ensuring equity when these resources are not fairly distributed (Fouad et al., 2006). Social justice is about fairness in the allocation of resources and opportunities among all people comprising a given society (Constantine et al., 2007; Cook, 1990) so that people who have less power will not be deprived (Prilleltensky, 2001) and will be equally able to engage in decision-making processes leading to action (Toporek et al., 2006). In short, a social justice perspective argues that all people should have equitable access to resources and that human rights must be protected. Therefore, structural and social inequalities should be minimized, and society should work toward the empowerment of people who belong to disadvantaged or disempowered groups.

In practice, promoting social justice involves an active attempt to change institutions, policies, and economic or governmental structures that perpetuate harmful or unfair practices that restrict access to resources (Fouad et al., 2006). It also involves changing the regularities of a system, or the way things are typically done (Sarason, 1981), so that fairness may be promoted and harm arising from standard organizational interventions or policies be prevented (Prilleltensky and Nelson, 2002).

Since public education is one of the main socialization mechanisms characterizing Western democracies, it is no wonder that much of the social justice debate focuses on the role of schools in determining fairness in the provision of educational services to children coming from different social groups. Schools should serve as sites for social amelioration in which social justice, an ideal of democracy, is practiced and cultivated (Adams, Bell, and Griffin, 2007). Public education should enable people to develop the critical analytical tools necessary to understand oppression and their own socialization within oppressive systems and to develop a sense of agency and capacity to oppose and change oppressive patterns and behaviors in themselves and in the institutions and communities in which they reside (Bell, 2007). Education systems that follow a social justice perspective should foster "equal participation of all groups in a society ... in which distribution of resources is equitable and all members are physically and psychologically safe and secure" (Bell, 2007, p. 1). Hence, schools should serve as sites of democracy with inherent ideological, cultural, religious, and social diversity and should strive toward social justice, a significant signpost of democracy.

While the ideal presented by the social justice approach should be embraced by everyone, and human rights should be protected everywhere, in practice this goal faces many obstacles undermining its realization. Achieving social justice seems to be difficult, in particular where illegal migrants are concerned. This last statement may be explained by considering that social justice argues for fairness and equitable allocation of bargaining powers, resources, and obligations for all members and groups comprising a society, whereas illegal migrants are frequently considered outsiders who are not entitled to the same rights that citizens have. Therefore, those attempting to provide equal rights to illegal migrants often face opposition from citizens who feel intimidated by the presence of foreigners.

This chapter tells the story of Bialik-Rogozin school, a remarkable school that has managed to beat the odds and create a warm, welcoming, and inspiring home for children of migrant families in spite of the many voices in Israeli society that have demanded their deportation.

The information presented in this chapter is based on an in-depth interview with Karen Tal, the Bialik-Rogozin school principal, and on an analysis of various documents including discussion protocols of the Israeli Parliament Committee established to monitor the problems of foreign workers, academic publications, and daily newspaper articles.

Although the ethical code for research implies that pseudo rather than real names should be utilized, this is not applicable in the current case since the name of the school, the principal, the teachers, and some of the children were mentioned in an Oscar-winning short documentary called *Strangers No More*.

The Bialik-Rogozin School

Before the Bialik-Rogozin school is described, some comments need to be made about the Israeli context and about the social and political atmosphere in which the school operates.

In 1948, the state of Israel was established as the homeland for the Jewish people. Israel's Nationality Law, enacted in 1952, grants citizenship to any Jewish person whether born in Israel or in any other place around the world as well as to non-Jewish people born in Israel before the Declaration of Independence. For the purpose of maintaining its Jewish character, a number of limitations are defined for non-Jewish individuals wishing to become Israeli citizens. According to these regulations, a person can apply for citizenship if his or her application meets six criteria: he or she currently lives in Israel; he or she has lived in Israel at least three of five years before the application is made; he or she is a permanent resident; he or she settled or intends to settle in Israel; he or she speaks Hebrew; he or she renounced his or her previous citizenship. Even if all six criteria are met, the final say is in the hands of the minister of interior, who tends to reject most applications in order to maintain a Jewish majority in the Israeli state.

Nevertheless, in recent years, many work migrants and refugees have entered the country legally or illegally. According to the Population and Immigration Authority, there are 37,885 refugees and work migrants currently living in Israel (Population and Immigration Authority, 2017). Since work opportunities are greater in the big cities located at the center, most migrants settle in the southern neighborhoods of Tel Aviv (The Israeli Parliament Committee, 2006), which are mostly populated by people of the lower socioeconomic groups. This has encouraged the locals to initiate violent protests against the migrants, arguing that the presence of migrants in their neighborhoods has a negative effect on their quality of life, creating greater difficulties than the ones they already experience.

Starting Point

The Bialik-Rogozin school is located in southern Tel Aviv and serves children of migrant families coming from forty-eight nationalities, children of Arab collaborators with the Israeli General Security Service, and Jewish children coming from families with low socioeconomic status. In 2005, 428 children studied at the school. The school is an amalgamation of two schools that have historically operated in the neighborhood: the Bialik elementary school, a traditional school where two hundred children coming mostly from work migrant families studied, and a few streets away, the Rogozin democratic high school that was about to be closed because of low registration. An engineer inspecting the Bialik school building directed that the school should be closed, and as a result, the municipality decided to merge the two schools and locate the Bialik elementary school in the Rogozin school building. The schools were located on separate floors and have their own administration and maintenance teams. The daily reality was characterized by frequent conflicts between children and teachers of the two schools.

When Karen was appointed the school principal of both schools, only two new students enrolled in the high school for the next school year, 28 percent of the graduates had obtained a matriculation diploma, and only 26 percent enlisted in the army. Discussions about closing down the school were already in process at the municipality. A visitor coming to the school couldn't overlook the chaos and neglect that characterized the place. As Karen describes,

> My first impression of the school was the strong smell that came out of the restrooms. Discussions at the municipality regarding the future of this school were in process, deterring any renovation initiatives or funds. The general atmosphere was characterized by lack of trust and despair. How can you expect children to succeed in an environment that does not respect them? How can you create a meaningful educational environment in a deteriorating building?

How can we succeed if the teachers don't believe in the children's ability to perform better academically? How can you create meaningful pedagogical processes for children who feel insecure because of their illegal status? I made up my mind: the two separated schools will be transformed into a unified campus with a shared teachers' room. I will turn this school into a pedagogical pearl in which respect is shared and granted to everyone. Better balance will be established between teachers' authority and responsibility.

In addition to the difficulties that followed the worsening condition of the school building, seven days after the school year had begun, an article opposing Karen's agenda and vision was published in a national newspaper by some of the teachers. These teachers wanted Karen's resignation so that old norms and habits allowing each teacher to act according to his or her individual discretion could be maintained. Karen recalls,

> I had the feeling that I am not a school principal but rather the manager of a trauma center where every minute a new dramatic event takes place. For example, there was a child who fainted on her first day in school. While I was calling for an ambulance, she woke up and started shouting hysterically: "Don't call: my mother will kill me if she has to pay for the ambulance." Every minute someone else opened my office door, notifying me about another dramatic event or disaster: one child was beating another; a teacher complaining that she cannot teach because the children don't have books; a teacher reporting that four students hadn't attended school for several days because the municipality was unwilling to subsidize their busing expenses since they live less than three kilometers away from school; a father of one child was deported by the immigration authorities; another was sent to prison . . . I remember that every evening after I left school, I used to sit in my car, think about all the tragic stories that I heard on that day, and cry. What can you tell a child whose mother was deported and he and his sister were left alone in a foreign country?

Karen

While this starting point could intimidate and scare away any rational person, for Karen it was the opposite. She perceived these circumstances as challenging and felt that the need to overcome this burden of difficulties advanced her motivation. Karen recalls some of her experiences as a child that created this attitude:

> I was born in Morocco. I came to Israel with my parents and brothers during the 1960s, and we settled in one of the low socioeconomic neighborhoods in Jerusalem. I met there many neglected children who everyone thought nothing

good could come out of them. My parents' motto was simple: we will work hard, and you will study and turn into a decent human being. My father worked as a mailman and waiter, and my parents saved every penny to buy us encyclopedias.

At home, we didn't used to conduct many conversations, and yet my parents always emphasized that we should strive to become honest and good people as our main goal in life. I went to high school, became an outstanding student, and was exposed to new ideas that opened my mind—to try to be the best, to never give up, and to always walk the extra mile. In the army I became a teacher-soldier and an officer and taught youngsters that came from underprivileged backgrounds.

The next thing I did after I was released from the army was to get higher education. One of my early childhood experiences which taught me never to be discouraged in the face of difficulties took place when I had to confront the neighborhood kids. There was a certain point when I decided that I would not be intimidated by the kids and that I was not willing to make a detour every time I wanted to walk from our building to the next one. So, on that day, I went out, passed next to the kids walking with my chin up, smiling. Although the kids made some remarks as I was passing by, that was the last time any of the kids bothered me.

Turning an Ugly Duckling into a Swan

Dealing with the highly complicated challenges facing the Bialik-Rogozin school would not be possible unless a clear strategy suitable for the school's particular circumstances was defined and supported by sufficient resources and infrastructure.

While some of the issues required the introduction of changes in the school's conduct and processes, other issues required the involvement of people or institutions operating in the school's organizational environment. Therefore, Karen's strategy reflects a combination of two complementary perspectives: one oriented inward and another oriented outward.

To decrease internal conflicts as much as possible, Karen introduced several structural changes. An initial step in this direction was to combine the two teacher rooms and create a vision that could be shared by all. In addition, the internal leadership was reorganized so that there was a continuum from kindergarten to twelfth grade, divided into "houses," each headed by a school staff member. Teachers chosen to serve as house leaders were those who showed more trust in Karen's vision:

> I realized that I would not be able to convince the teachers who wrote about me in the newspaper article asking for my resignation. This would take all my

attention and energy. There was another group of teachers that were silent, waiting to see what would happen. However, there was a third relatively small group of teachers—those who expressed interest in my ideas and were willing to take an active part in the adventure.

House leaders later became members of the extended school managing board responsible for setting school policies: "In our board meetings we discussed, debated, and even quarreled over a variety of issues, but once a decision was made, everyone was committed to disseminate it among the rest of the teachers and to ensure its implementation."

To allow each house to operate autonomously and provide immediate solutions to difficulties and problems, the role of each of the two school counselors was redefined so that they could work closely with each house leader: "There was too much talking about problems and difficulties and not enough actions taken in order to have these problems solved."

To promote professional discussions and extend the discourse on academic standards and expectations, a two-hour time slot was created in the program where the house leaders, counselors, and teachers teaching in that house met on a weekly basis. These meetings "were a major part of the mechanism created to better balance authority with responsibility and accountability and to turn the teachers from social workers to pedagogical professionals."

Teachers' and students' tendency to come late to school was another aspect that had a significant negative impact on the school's culture and atmosphere and therefore had to be changed. "It really bothers me when someone doesn't come on time," says Karen. "This is something that my parents emphasized. When you don't come on time, you don't respect the others. I couldn't stand the fact that children had to wait in the classroom for a teacher who was late." To eliminate this bad habit and encourage teachers and students to come to school on time, Karen used to stand every morning at the school entrance and say hello to everyone coming in.

> When I made this decision, I wasn't aware of the additional benefits that might come out of it. Standing every morning at the school gate exposed me to the children who come to school on a rainy day without a coat or in shorts; I noticed that when I smile to the children, some smile back while others enter quickly with a sad look on their faces. It enabled me to better locate the children in distress.

Since many of the schoolchildren come from migrant families that struggle every day in order to survive, it became obvious that focusing the attention on students' academic performance while neglecting the other aspects of their daily reality might be misleading. Therefore, some action had to be taken to allow school staff to better understand each student's unique needs and home circumstances. Karen confesses, "I know I have many deficiencies, but among my advantages is my ability to ask for assistance when I am not sure how something needs to be done."

Hence, Karen contacted a faculty member at one of the universities who specializes in special education, and he taught the school staff how to perform a "multidimensional mapping" for each student. This mapping looked at the children's academic performance as well as their emotional state, health and well-being, and the welfare of their families. Next, instead of focusing on the many problems that this mapping process detects, the professor suggested looking for the points of strength characterizing each child and focusing on them. "This mapping created a work plan for each child," Karen summarizes.

The Executive Council

In addition to the activities intended to transform the teachers' professional conduct and attitude and the school's culture and atmosphere, many of the problems and challenges related to the unique school population required negotiation with external institutions that were not part of the educational hierarchy. Hence, such capacity had to be established.

In search of a mechanism that could serve as a source of support and backup for the school, Karen decided to create an executive council. This forum was composed of powerful people in the Israeli society who volunteered to be part of the council and assist in the various issues that the school had to confront based on their abilities, connections, and expertise.

The council was composed of businesspeople and leaders in Israeli industry, judges, politicians, municipal officials, and others representing various institutions and organizations operating in areas of relevance.

Promoting a sense of protectiveness among the children was one of the first challenges that faced council members. This may be understood by considering that many of them, including those who were born in Israel, were not considered citizens by the Israeli authorities and, therefore, could be deported at any time. Karen says,

> I read the children's rights convention, which states in the second paragraph that every child is entitled to health care, welfare, and education. If children that come in the morning to school are not sure that they will have a home to which they can return to by the end of the day, what is the point in trying to teach them mathematics or language?

It was brought to Karen's attention that the birth certificates provided to work migrants' children who were born is Israel stated "live newborn" rather than "Israeli citizen" to indicate their temporary status. Hence, Karen asked a few lawyers who were part of the executive council to try to have this changed. They prepared a petition in which they raised various legal and moral claims, arguing that the formal status of these children should be changed and supporting their claims with evidence indicating the children's mastery of the Hebrew language and their social and cultural relatedness to Israeli society.

One of the council members who was a close friend of the prime minister's wife made sure that she would receive the petition. Karen recalls, "I used to tell the children that we are doing everything that is in our power to prevent their deportation, but we cannot promise that we will succeed." A few months later, the issue was raised at a cabinet meeting, and the formal status of non-Jewish children born in Israel was temporarily changed.

Realizing that the school's unique population has many needs and difficulties that go beyond pedagogic and didactic issues and based on the growing number of volunteers who became part of the executive council, Karen decided to establish a "round table" forum in which all relevant stakeholders participated. This forum was composed of parents, teachers, and lawyers, faculty members from academia, physicians, high-ranking army officers, and representatives of the main social organizations operating in Israel. The variety of the members and their connections with influential people in various spheres of Israeli society enabled them to cope with almost any issue that came up.

The school's absorption of refugees from Darfur serves as a typical example of the challenges that faced members of the round table. On the last day of the 2008 summer vacation, Karen received a phone call from the municipality, asking her if the school was capable and willing to accept twenty-eight refugee children who had escaped from Darfur.

> I immediately responded that I would be happy to absorb these children into our school, but then I realized that I know very little about them. I was told that they all were staying in a church nearby. I went there and couldn't believe my eyes. The smell was awful. Approximately two hundred people were laying on the ground—men, women, children; in one corner there was a huge pile of clothes donated by Israeli citizens and the municipality. But what amazed me most was the silence: it was the silence of despair.

On the next day, the children came to school. Karen recalls that most of them had never attended school. Some of them wouldn't stop running in the corridors; others just sat on their own. Communication became a problem because there was hardly anyone in school who spoke their language. While the entire school staff was engaged in the effort to absorb these children into the school in the best way possible, a new problem beyond their professional capacity arose. It turned out that these children had never been vaccinated. Karen recalls,

> Among the members of our round table was a physician who held a position in one of the major hospitals in town. I called her and asked for her assistance. She made some inquiries, and two hours later she called me back with the following message: make sure you have their parents' signed approval, prepare a room in school, and provide a staff member to manage the process. Within twenty-four hours, all of the children were vaccinated.

Enriching School Activities

The resources that the school formally received from the Ministry of Education and the municipality could not satisfy the extent of the needs that characterized the school's unique community. It was clear that the school had to become the main anchor in the lives of the children and their families. Bearing this thought in mind, Karen, with the support of the executive council members, decided to set up a volunteer-based team to enrich the children's daily experiences in school. Each council member contacted his or her friends, asking them to assist. Karen recalls, "The only thing that guided us were the children's needs. My dream was to open school from early morning until late evening so that in the morning the children could study, at noon lunch would be served, and, in the afternoon, they would be able to enjoy various enrichment activities."

Sure enough, a variety of activities began. Sixty-four soldiers who served in a prestigious military intelligence unit volunteered to assist the children; a senior official from the Ministry of Commerce taught the children a course about software inspection; following a connection established with the Cisco company, some of the children became the managers of Internet forums. An eighty-year-old pensioner volunteered to help children who needed special assistance; a connection with the medicine faculty at the university was established, and some of the students volunteered in school as part of their medical training; another volunteer offered a course in juggling; one of the major Israeli sports clubs offered sports activities in the afternoon. Karen says,

We had to articulate and enforce a procedure to ensure that all volunteers had no criminal backgrounds and that every volunteer would have a contact person to whom he or she could apply. Every house leader was responsible for the variety of activities provided to the children in her house . . . you can't centrally run such a complicated network of activities: you must delegate authority to others if you want things to happen.

Looking Holistically: The Parents

Fear and uncertainty are among the daily experiences that illegal migrant families share. In 2011, these fears were aggravated following the appointment of a new minister of interior. This minister, who came from a religious political party, stated that all illegal work migrants should be deported. Although the police stated that no arrests would take place in school, on the days that followed this declaration, migrant children did not come to school, and the streets that were usually crowded with migrant adults remained empty.

In spite of the efforts invested by the executive council members and the governmental decisions that temporarily extended the stay of migrant children born in Israel, these decisions failed to provide a permanent solution for the children and their families.

Hence, it was clear that the school's efforts to advance the children would only produce limited results unless substantial assistance were to be provided to their parents. With this in mind, Karen and the teachers decided to act.

Initially, they prepared a letter to the parents containing a single sentence: "What can our school do for you?" This sentence was then translated into as many languages as possible, and each student was asked to bring it home and return it to school a few days later. Not all the parents responded, but those who did wrote "learn Hebrew." They also asked that studies take place on Sundays because this was their day off.

An invitation to participate in a Hebrew study group addressed to the parents was disseminated among the children, stating that the following Sunday at 18:00 the first lesson would begin. Karen describes it:

> The next Sunday came. I remember sitting in my office in a meeting. I didn't think that anyone would show up, so we didn't make any preparations. I decided to stay in school until 19:00 to be on the safe side. However, a few minutes after 18:00, I heard loud noise coming from the corridor. I stepped out of my office and saw a crowd of parents standing and waiting for their first Hebrew lesson. I opened our assembly hall, used my teaching and improvisation skills, and asked the parents about their names, places of birth, and their dates of birth.

Then, I taught them how to sing "Happy Birthday" in Hebrew, Spanish, Arabic, and English. After forty minutes I apologized and said that I was embarrassed because I had not expected them to come. I promised that next week we would start our lessons in groups of twenty. I also said that we would provide instructors who would play with their children during lesson time so that mothers would be free to learn.

The next Sunday, 128 parents showed up. Parents' trust in the school was established when parents realized that the teachers and I talk the talk and walk the walk. This led later on to additional activities and workshops in which parents told stories about their home countries, about their religion, and proper ways to educate children were discussed.

Gaining Recognition

In light of the growing social protest against work migrants and the official policy to deport non-Jewish migrants guided by the newly elected minister of interior, it was clear that gaining recognition for the school might play a crucial role in determining the quality and amount of resources that the school would receive and, therefore, its capacity to offer rich and meaningful services to its community.

One step in this direction was the establishment of a school choir. In addition to the choir's contribution to the children's musical education, it created an opportunity for the school to present visitors with the children singing in Hebrew and smiling rather than highlighting their misery: "No one can listen to the choir singing and remain indifferent" (Tamir, 2011, p. 122).

A sports team was another initiative that allowed the children to prove their skill to outsiders. It was also a channel used to decrease tensions that arose from time to time among children coming from different nationalities. During the Purim holiday, a member of the executive council suggested conducting a costume parade in the neighborhood instead of having an indoor celebration. The police authorized the event and provided police officers who maintained security and blocked the traffic. The children dressed in costumes and marched in the streets with the city mayor walking at the front. Karen describes the event: "The children, the police band, and some of the policemen who were considered by the children as the 'bad people' coming to arrest them marched together in the streets in broad daylight. It was an amazing experience for the children, for the police officers, for the school staff, and for the people living in the neighborhood."

Another element in the school's strategy aimed at gaining recognition was evident in the large number of highly influential people who visited the school. In one incident, Martin Luther King, III came for a visit; in another, it was the prime minister who came to the school. The Israeli president also came for a visit and wrote in the school's visitors' album: "This is a school that serves as a home for its children, a school that gives hope to every child and the right to be equal and different at the same time."

Beating the Odds

We live in an era in which any discussion about education seems incomplete unless hard evidence based on conventional indicators testifying to school effectiveness is provided. This premise seems to hold true universally, regardless of the unique challenges characterizing individual schools.

Although the Bialik-Rogozin school has had to cope with many challenges that go beyond academic assignments and goals, looking at the school from a school effectiveness perspective reveals amazing accomplishments. At the time the two schools were united under Karen's leadership, 428 children coming from forty-eight countries studied in the school. Only 28 percent of the graduates received a matriculation diploma, and only 26 percent of them enlisted in the army. Six years later, 789 children studied in the school (Tal, 2011), 87 percent of the graduates received a matriculation diploma, and 79 percent enlisted in the army.

Although these accomplishments put the Bialik-Rogozin school in the high-performing schools category, these figures fail to tell the real story, a story of a principal and a group of teachers determined to bring change against all odds to the lives of migrant children. These numbers fail to reflect school staff's constant exposure to multifaceted struggles between values and agendas, between different perceptions of right and wrong, between motivations and possibilities, between "us" and "others."

While any attempt to promote social justice in a diversified society is tough, promoting social justice for individuals who live in an unwelcoming social and political atmosphere while lacking citizenship seems like an impossible task. And yet, the story of the Bialik-Rogozin school suggests that a few committed and steadfast people headed by a devoted school leader can beat the deterministic and self-fulfilling prophesy and create an educational microcosm shaped by dignity, respect, and humaneness.

After six years characterized by constant battles, Karen decided to move on. She is now heading a nonprofit organization aimed at creating a managerial and professional platform for schools operating at the social periphery in Israel and turning them into a source of inspiration for their communities.

At the end of our interview, I couldn't resist asking Karen why she chose to leave the Bialik-Rogozin school. She replied,

> Staying in the school was the reasonable and easy thing to do: everything was working smoothly; it became an autopilot type of leadership. However, it was always clear to me: this is not *my* school. I am just a messenger, and I had to make sure that I would not be motivated by my hubris. It was the right time for me to leave and let others continue what I started.

References

Adams, M., Bell, L. A., and Griffin, P. (2007). *Teaching for diversity and social justice*. New York, NY: Routledge.

Bell, L. A. (2007). Theoretical foundations for social justice education. In M. Adams, L. A. Bell, and P. Griffin (Eds.). *Teaching for diversity and social justice*, New York, NY: Routledge.

Constantine, M. G., Hage, S. M., Kindaichi, M. M., and Bryant, R. M. (2007). Social justice and multicultural issues: Implications for the practice and training of counselors and counseling psychologists. *Journal of Counseling and Development*, 85(1), 24–29.

Cook, S. W. (1990). Toward a psychology of improving justice: Research on extending the equality principle to victims of social injustice. *Journal of Social Issues*, 46(1), 147–61.

Fouad, N., Gerstein, L. H., Toporek, R. L., Roysircar, G., and Israel, T. (2006). Social justice and counseling psychology in context. In R. L. Toporek, L. H. Gerstein, N. A. Fouad, G. Roysircar, and T. Israel (Eds.), *Handbook for social justice in counseling psychology: Leadership, vision, and action* (pp. 1–15). Thousand Oaks, CA: Sage.

International Labour Organization. (2015). *Mainstreaming of migration in development policy and integrating migration in the post-2015 UN development agenda*. Retrieved from www.ilo.org/global/topics/labour-migration/publications/WCMS_220084/lang--en/index.htm.

Population and Immigration Authority. (2017). *Data on foreigners in Israel*. The Department for Planning and Policy no. 2017/3, October 2, 2017. Retrieved from https://www.gov.il/BlobFolder/generalpage/foreign_workers_stats/he/foreign_workers_stats_q3_2017_0.pdf.

Prilleltensky, I. (2001). Value-based praxis in community psychology: Moving towards social justice and social action. *American Journal of Community Psychology*, 29(5), 747–78.

Prilleltensky, I., and Nelson, G. (2002). *Doing psychology critically: Making a difference in diverse settings*. Houndmills, UK: Palgrave MacMillan.

Sarason, S. (1981). An asocial psychology and a misdirected clinical psychology. *American Psychologist*, 36(8), 827–36.

Tal, K. (2011). Multiplicity is the true magic. In S. Govrin (Ed.), *Seeing the voices: Human and educational complexity in Israeli schools from the principals' point of view* (pp. 105–14). Kfar-Saba, Israel: Ovnaim (in Hebrew).

Tamir, Y. (2011). They don't have another country. In S. Govrin (Ed.), *Seeing the voices: Human and educational complexity in Israeli schools from the principals' point of view* (pp. 118–22). Kfar-Saba, Israel: Ovnaim (in Hebrew).

The Israeli Parliament Committee. (2006). *Tracking the problems of foreign workers: A protocol of a meeting conducted at the Israeli Parliament on August 29th, 2006 (Hebrew)*. Retrieved from www.aisrael.org/_Uploads/37132006-08-29.rtf.

Toporek, R. L., Williams, R., Gerstein, L. H., Fouad, N. A., Roysircar, G., and Israel, T. (2006). Ethics and professional issues related to the practice of social justice in counseling psychology. In R. L. Toporek, L. H. Gerstein, N. A. Fouad, G. Roysircar, and T. Israel (Eds.), *Handbook for social justice in counseling psychology: Leadership, vision, and action* (pp. 17–34). Thousand Oaks, CA: Sage.

UNHCR—The UN Refugee Agency. (2016). *Global trends: Forced displacement in 2015*. Retrieved from http://www.unhcr.org/statistics/unhcrstats/576408cd7/unhcr-global-trends-2015.html.

CHAPTER TWO

School Leadership to Increase Inclusive Education Practices in China, Thailand, and Turkey

Tanyathorn Hauwadhanasuk, Min Zhuang,
Susan Toft Everson, PhD, Shenggang Yu, PhD,
and Mustafa Karnas, PhD

In the United States, Public Law 94–142 was passed in 1975 with the aim "to insure that for every child with disability there will be a tailor-made program reflecting the effort to maximize that child's participation in the classroom's and school's 'normal' activities" (Sarason, 1996, p. 235). Since that time, educational approaches to implement the law have evolved and have been institutionalized into the system. "By the 1980s and 1990s, the interpretation evolved into the approach now known as *inclusion*: the principle and practice of considering general education as the placement of first choice for all learners" (Villa and Thousand, 2003, p. 1).

Now, the inclusion of students with disabilities into the everyday life of classrooms and schools is common in the United States and is growing in many other countries. This reform initiative has moved beyond the familiar story of the United States to become an international story, which provides the examples for this chapter. Using this context of inclusion as the reform initiative, this chapter focuses first on a brief description of leadership associated with making and implementing planned change through comprehensive educational reform initiatives.

Such leadership is integral to continuous improvement, including the implementation and improvement of inclusion programs. The next section describes three examples of the development of inclusion systems and practices, including the role of leaders in that work. These research studies occurred outside the United States and were based in China, Thailand, and Turkey. Finally, the chapter's conclusion addresses the common elements among the sections and offers some suggestions for practices that emerged from the example countries.

Leadership for Planned Change

The administrator plays a key role in the success of efforts at inclusion. Villa and Thousand delineated five essential actions administrators must take to facilitate inclusive practices:

1. Building consensus for vision of inclusive schooling;
2. Developing educators with the skills and confidence to be inclusive educators through ongoing professional development;
3. Creating incentives such as time, training, responding to concerns and recognition;
4. Reorganizing and expanding human and other teaching resources; and
5. Planning for and taking actions to help the community see and get excited about a new vision. (As cited in Cordeiro and Cunningham, 2013, p. 339.)

These are the actions of educators who effectively lead *planned* change and continuous school improvement. The concept of planned change is important to the work described in this chapter. Initiating a comprehensive program for inclusion requires planned change. Change in education is inevitable and unpredictable; planned change is intentional and includes reasoned, evidenced-based, smart decisions (Fullan, 2001). Over time, the reliance on research-based practices has become an essential ingredient in educational reform.

According to Block (2000), one common component of leading comprehensive educational reform initiatives is "effective, research-based methods and strategies" (p. 7). What is it leaders do when they lead educational change? In an early important long-term study of educational change agent behaviors, Miles, Saxl, and Lieberman (1988) identified five characteristics of effective change agents: they build trust and rapport, use organizational diagnosis, deal with the process, use resources, and manage the work.

This early work guided leadership training and development over time. Still, even with knowledge and training tied to these practices, leading educational change effectively is not and has never been easy. "One reason that leadership itself is such a challenging professional and person responsibility is that effective leadership requires a continuous engagement in moving individuals and organizations from their present state to the leader's vision of an ideal state, and the movement requires change" (Reeves, 2006, p. 99).

Other studies have focused on effective school-level leadership, where educational change and school reform initiatives are implemented. For example, Marzano, Waters, and McNulty (2005), in a meta-analysis of educational leadership studies, identified twenty-five responsibilities of school leaders and clarified their connection to *first-order change*, which is incremental, and *second-order change*, which is deep system change (for example, see Argyris and Schön, 1974, 1978; Cuban, 1987; Fullan, 2001). Inclusion reform initiatives are system changes of the second order.

In addition, it is important to note that systems change is complicated by the interaction of the system's domains. "While the nature of each domain influences an educator's actions, including those that guide change, the interaction of domains also exerts considerable influence on change activities" (Everson, 2000, p. 384). Because of this complexity, changes in educational inclusion have been slow in coming and difficult to lead.

In 1996, Sarason revisited his early work on school culture and educational change. In it, he focused on the issues of serving students with special needs, an important topic to him. After he provided serious critiques regarding progress, he identified two basic criteria for school change. "The imagery conveyed by these critiques and programs is imagery of social contexts in a school in which the behavioral regularities of children and teachers are obviously different in quality and quantity than they are now. It is imagery capable of being systemically and rigorously evaluated" (Sarason, 1996, p. 361).

These social contexts in which leaders guide new inclusion programs have notable power. This is particularly challenging when addressing the implementation of inclusion programs in the different social contexts within each country. Adding to the complexity is the power of culture. The effectiveness of the leadership actions listed above may also be influenced by the culture in which the leader works to initiate an educational inclusion program.

In the GLOBE Study of sixty-two societies, researchers found some leadership characteristics to be universal, such as trustworthy, planful, positive, motivating, decisive, and intelligent, as well as not unfriendly, irritable, or self-centered. Others, such as being autonomous, ambitious, cunning, intuitive, logical, and risk-taking, were valued more highly in some cultures than others (as cited in Bolman and Deal, 2017, p. 339). Overall, preparing and developing leaders to guide this complex school change work is daunting.

Two recent dissertations point to principals' perceptions that they generally lack the preparation and support to lead special education programs (Keenoy, 2012; Schulze, 2014). Using Villa and Thousand's five essential actions for leaders of inclusion programs may only be a first step. Understanding educational change, culture, and context and their interaction will be essential to substantive leadership preparation and development program designs. Educational leaders need to use direction and alignment to build a culture of visionaries, to encourage risk-taking and experimentation, to set the pace, and to lead by example.

Principals must discuss and translate knowledge and research for excellent schools. The spark of individual and group genius required to really make a difference in education must be ignited (Cordeiro and Cunningham, 2013, p. 95). In general, new, helpful ideas about how to support educational system change are emerging. For example, Fullan and Quinn (2016) and Leithwood (2019), experts who focus on leading educational reform, published books addressing the work of large-scale and system change and the leadership that is needed to guide such change.

Fullan and Quinn introduced the concept of using the "right drivers" to guide system change. They wrote, "We are seeing a growing interest in policy and practice in embracing the right drivers' framework from countries, states, provinces, districts, and schools" (2016, p. 11). In the summary to his book, Leithwood (2019) provided "Eleven Lessons About Effective Project Leadership" (p. 156). These focus on the leadership of large-scale improvement processes. Such ideas can enhance the leadership of inclusion reform around the world.

Examples of Roles of Leaders in Three Countries

China: The Context of Inclusive Education

Policy and Practice in China

The United Nations Educational Scientific and Cultural Organization (UNESCO) convened an Asian-Pacific regional conference on special education in 1993 and issued the Harbin Declaration at the same meeting (Huang, 2004). Following the declaration's mandate, inclusive education in China has made rapid progress (Fang, 2009). This commitment deepens Chinese educators' concept of inclusive education and also helps to shape educational policy through the form of legislation in order to promote inclusive education (Fang, 2009).

Under such a scenario, Chinese educators started to focus more on inclusive education. According to the search results from the National Library of China and China National Knowledge Infrastructure, as of April 2018, there were 2,034 articles with the theme of inclusive education. By referencing the experience from international practice, Chinese educators try to construct an inclusive education mode that conforms to the national conditions of China.

Research topics within this field include but are not limited to the localization of inclusive education (Peng, 1994; B. Wang, 2012; J. Wang, 2002; Xu, Sun, and Lei, 2010), social awareness (Huang, 2001), teachers' perspectives (Deng, 2008; Mu, et al., 2015), curriculum adaptation for inclusive education (Li, 2016; Xiao, 2007), and policy support (Zhao, 2010). Learning in Regular Classroom (LRC) is a government-supported schooling mode for students with disabilities that aims to fulfill the requirements of students with special needs in mainstream educational institutions (Deng and Manset, 2000; Xiao, 2005).

This mode not only represents the Western concept of inclusive education but also adheres to localization of inclusion, and it facilitates the popularity of compulsory education among students with disabilities (Mu et al., 2015; Xiao, 2005). Humanity, care, and charity are China's traditional cultural values that led to the development of LRC (Xu, Cooper, and Sin, 2018). However, the educational equity and high quality of the LRC cannot only rely on humanity, care, or charity (Xu, Cooper, and Sin, 2018).

According to Xu, Cooper, and Sin, "It was because mainstream teachers' care and love have not yet evolved into effective teaching pedagogy or strategies for students with disabilities in their classroom" (2018, p. 67). In 2015, there were approximately 440,000 students with disabilities enrolled in schools; over half of them were studying in regular classrooms (关于完善残疾儿童随班就读政策的提案 [*Proposal for improving the policy of children with disabilities in regular classroom*], 2017).

The mode of LRC would support students with disabilities, such as helping them integrate into communities and developing their social adaptability, among other roles (关于完善残疾儿童随班就读政策的提案 [*Proposal for improving the policy of children with disabilities in regular classroom*], 2017). But LRC may be associated with some other issues, such as high dropout rates among students with disabilities or teachers' disregard for students with disabilities (Mu et al., 2015).

Examination-oriented education, which highlights mutual comparison and competition, has been deeply rooted in the Chinese educational system (Xu, Cooper, and Sin, 2018). Xu and colleagues (2018) noted, "This overemphasis on examination scores overlooks each citizen's need for personal development and leads to the fact that educational success becomes privilege for a minority of 'winners' at the expense of the majority and the weak" (p. 67). Teachers may not be able to meet the needs of students with disabilities (Xiao, 2007).

In other words, examination-oriented education limits initiative and the participation of teachers in teaching students with disabilities (Mu et al., 2015). Besides, due to the policy issues, newly qualified special education teachers can hardly become mainstream teachers in regular schools (Xu, Cooper, and Sin, 2018). Multidisciplinary teams (including school psychologists, therapists, etc.), on the other hand, are generally unavailable for LRC (Xu, Cooper, and Sin, 2018). Therefore, students with disabilities are more likely to fail in this system (Xu, Cooper, and Sin, 2018).

Special Education Program Overview

According to previous research, administrators faced challenges during the process of promoting LRC in China. One of the big challenges of implementation was that LRC could only satisfy students with vision disabilities, hearing disabilities, and/or mild or moderate intellectual disabilities (Deng and Jing, 2013). LRC would not benefit every student with a disability. Another challenge was the lack of supporting systems in identification, classification, and assessment of students with disabilities (关于完善残疾儿童随班就读政策的提案 [*Proposal for improving the policy of children with disabilities in regular classroom*], 2017).

In addition to the issues of policy implementation, schools may not be able to provide essential support to promote inclusive education; students with disabilities would become more vulnerable to this unsound educational mode (关于完善残疾儿童随班就读政策的提案 [*Proposal for improving the policy of children with disabilities in regular classroom*], 2017). Mu and colleagues (2015) cited that teacher beliefs, skills, and knowledge play important roles in providing a conceptual framework for teachers to have professional competence for LRC practices.

Teacher resources are the precondition for inclusive education to realize its comprehensive and fundamental function. Teachers' agency, for instance, consciously and constantly motivated teachers to seek more resources to help students with disabilities and implement LRC (Mu et al., 2015). Therefore, classroom management is an important aspect of promoting inclusive education in China.

In order to know teachers' attitudes toward inclusive education, previous research has studied general education teachers' perspectives on admitting students with disabilities. The results indicated that 39.6 percent of the teachers were negative or skeptical about mainstream schools' capabilities of teaching students with disabilities; 82.6 percent were worried that they would not get a sense of achievement from teaching students with disabilities, and 81.8 percent thought they were not competent to implement inclusive education (Liu, Du, and Yao, 2000).

Furthermore, most of the teachers agreed with inclusive education. However, there was a big difference in teachers' attitudes toward inclusion between urban and rural areas. More specifically, teachers who were from urban areas were more likely to have negative attitudes toward inclusive education (Deng, 2008). In terms of teacher education, training programs for instructors are inadequate. With regard to inclusive education, before-position training is weak in the variability of program design; the training system must improve (Jiang, Wu, and Du, 2017).

On the other hand, post-position training lacks relevant programs to apply theories and practices for inclusive education (Jiang, Wu, and Du, 2017). There are several serious impediments to professional development among inclusive education teachers, including imperfect legal and policy systems and the shortage of funding and technical support (Jiang, Wu, and Du, 2017).

Special Education Leadership Research Examples

In academia, some researchers have argued that it is not necessary for Chinese educational institutions to place more emphasis on accepting students with disabilities into regular schools (Lei, 2015). They explained that if students with disabilities will not get benefits from regular schools, their academic performance will be worse than if they enroll in special education schools (Lei, 2015). Having students with special needs physically present in regular classes does not mean teachers or peers fully accept them socially and psychologically; students with special needs may still have to deal with issues of discrimination (Huang, 2014).

In order to know middle and high school principals' perceptions of inclusive education in China, four principals and three teachers were interviewed by an educational leader of the School of Education at Beihua University. Two principals said, "We hope inclusive education can be fully implemented in China. School education should be inclusive of everyone and benefit all the students' needs. However, due to the low economic levels in China, we only can do limited things to improve teacher resource and educational facilities" (S. Yu, personal communication, April 2018).

One high school teacher said, "Now we have LGBTQ students, they are rejected by teachers and peers. I think how to accept them is a part of inclusive education" (S. Yu, personal communication, April 2018). The common opinion from principals and teachers has been that inclusive education might only be implemented at the elementary level. The Chinese secondary education system is based on exam-oriented education, and students are under great pressure to pursue further education (S. Yu, personal communication, April 2018).

If students have differences in intelligence, it will be difficult for them to merge in the class. Therefore, students with special needs may be isolated or rejected by their peers. On the other hand, schools may not have the ability to apply the universal design in schools' facilities, such as barrier-free paths and barrier-free bathrooms (S. Yu, personal communication, April 2018). To this end, the educational leaders must take actions to value theoretical research, to reform policy and teaching practices, to upgrade facilities and resources for teaching, and to meet the special education laws and regulations in order to promote inclusive education.

Thailand: The Context of Inclusive Education

Policy and Practice in Thailand

The government policy has moved toward "education for all," and a constitution for the people's right to education was enacted in 1999 with an implementation of the National Education Act. The purpose of this act was to provide equal opportunity for every child (Kantavong, Nethanomsak, and Luang-ungkool, 2012). The Education for All policy resulted in an increase of school rate attendance in 2009 (Ministry of Education [MoE], 2015).

With a focus on raising learner achievement in all schools, results on the national test of basic curriculum content had shown improvement in learner achievement going from scores of 75.93 to 86 from 2008 through 2013 (MoE, 2015, p. 80). Government policy stipulated the Constitution of 2007 on the Compulsory Education Act of 1992 to provide the right to access from nine to twelve years of a quality basic education at no cost, which resulted in an increase in attaining a primary and secondary education (MoE, 2015).

According to Tangkitvanich and Sasiwuttiwat (2012), it is critical that the quality of Thai education be improved in terms of utilization of educational resources, pedagogy, curriculum, and assessment system. Comprehensive implementation must focus on student-centered learning, funding allocation to disadvantaged schools, and effective in-service teacher training (Fry and Bi, 2013). The researchers suggested that educational leaders in Thailand must utilize the spending of educational resources and focus funding allocations toward the most disadvantaged schools (Fry and Bi, 2013).

Importantly, education spending must emphasize developing effective in-service teacher training and recruiting people to the field of teaching at all levels in order to enhance teaching quality. Although issues of inequality and inequity in the Thai education system exist, the Thai educational research database on these issues was enhanced to a great extent to inform educational decision making. It is necessary for Thailand to improve the quality of education and to decrease regional disparities (Fry and Bi, 2013).

A few studies by Fry, Nattapoj, and Wannapa and Supinda showed that the quality of education provided for children was an indicator of the future of Thailand (as cited in Fry and Bi, 2013). According to Fry and Bi (2013), the analysis of policy found that the Ministry of Education had promoted the Education for All policy; as a result, a number of universities integrated the skill set necessary for understanding and teaching practices based on human rights into special education and inclusive education programs (Kantavong, Nethanomsak, and Luang-ungkool, 2012).

Special Education Program Attribute

Thailand's National Education Act of 1999 mandated every school to provide opportunities for children with disabilities, regardless of severity, to be included in the general education programs (Fulk, Swerdlik, and Kosuwan, 2002). The Office of Basic Education Commission of Bureau of Special Education developed educational programs in special needs schools and welfare schools to ensure equal access for diverse learners (MoE, 2015, p. 22). In addition, there were some other programs and activities created to support and promote basic education for children who are disadvantaged, who are disabled, and who are from ethnic minority groups. These programs included Home as Classroom, Parent as Teacher; implementation of the Waldorf bilingual approach to improve instruction for children who are deaf; professional development programs to improve the quality of special education teachers; and an inclusive education project to improve instructions for children with learning disabilities (MoE, 2015, p. 23).

In response to the Education for All policy, in-service teacher training programs have been offered. For example, knowledge of early intervention, characteristics of children with disabilities, behavior management, and teaching instructions and approaches have been promoted (Fulk, Swerdlik, and Kosuwan, 2002). Due to in-service teacher training limitations and inadequate resource allocation, teachers were unprepared to teach students with disabilities (Carter, 2006).

The in-service teaching institutions offer special education and inclusive education courses to develop teacher attitudes toward individuals with disabilities (Kantavong, Nethanomsak, and Luang-ungkool, 2012). In terms of teacher training curricula and material, areas of improvement include knowledge, attitudes, behaviors, skills, content of textbooks, and pedagogy, and teacher guides were required (Kantavong, Nethanomsak, and Luangungkook, 2012).

As Thailand aimed to achieve the goal of Education for All, researchers made efforts to implement the professional learning (PL) programs to prepare educational stakeholders (teachers, principals, students, and families) with effective inclusive education programs (Kantavong and Sivabaedya, 2010). The content of the PL programs was designed to focus on the intervention techniques and to address the concept of inclusive education with effective interventions for students with disabilities in three categories: students with autism spectrum disorder (ASD), students with attention deficit hyperactivity disorder (ADHD), and students with learning disability (LD) (Kantavong and Sivabaedya, 2010).

Researchers indicated that the PL programs for in-service training teachers enhanced the learning of students with ASD, ADHD, and LD in inclusive classrooms; in addition, teachers gained hands-on experiences and confidence to develop their own teaching practices (Kantavong and Sivabaedya, 2010).

Special Education Leadership Research Example

From policy to practice, Thai classroom teachers are expected to have skills and knowledge to support the needs of students with disabilities that will promote students' learning to reach their potential (Opartkiattikul, Arthur-Kelly, and Dempsey, 2014). The mixed-methods study conducted by Fry and Bi (2013) indicated the success of most structural and legal changes on the educational system of Thailand as well as challenges for Thailand to achieve its educational potential, including human resource development.

Studies by Fry, Bovornsiri, and Uampuang; Murata; and Raktham indicated that "both Thai culture in general, and political culture in particular have made an impact on the implementation of educational reform" (as cited in Fry and Bi, 2013, p. 291). Bermani (2017) investigated the extent to which principals' leadership and decision-making processes exerted influences on the operations of inclusive classrooms. This study revealed that the principals did not apply their knowledge of instructional planning and strategies, effective instructions, collaborative decision making, governance, and technology into their practices.

The study by Bermani (2017) showed that principals did not have the experience or training and relied heavily on consultants, specialists, and teachers to make decisions for students on the autism spectrum in elementary inclusion classrooms. Yell, Drasgow, and Lowrey (2005) noted that principals may have little to no preparatory experience in special education to support both general education and special education teachers as well as co-teaching in the inclusive classroom.

The ethnographic research conducted by Grimes (2013) at two schools in Bangkok, Thailand, between 2003 and 2009 indicated significant barriers regarding teacher development for inclusion. These barriers included the culture of school leaders and teachers and the leaders' support for teachers to take ownership of their own development in the school and classroom at their own pace. Implications for the development of inclusive teachers addressed that successful policy initiatives must enable teachers and educational stakeholders to work in collaboration for constructive dialogues and reflections (Grimes, 2013).

Turkey: Special Education Program Description

Policy and Practice in Turkey

The Ministry of National Education undertakes fundamental duties in the provision of educational services (Ministry of National Education, 2005) with the general aim of "promoting the welfare and happiness of the citizens and society; supporting and accelerate economic, cultural and social development in national unity and cohesion; and making the nation constructive and distinguished partner of contemporary civilization" (p. 17).

According to the Basic Law of National Education of 1973, the Turkish national education system aims to "raise highly skillful, productive and creative individuals of the Information Age who are committed to Atatürk's principles and revolution, have advanced thinking and problem-solving skills, are committed to democratic values and open to new ideas, have feelings of personal responsibility, have assimilated the national culture, can interpret different cultures and contribute to modern civilization, and lean towards productive science and technology" (*World Data on Education*, 2012, p. 2).

Turkey has encountered challenges in the education system from the rapid increase in population, migration from rural to urban areas, and budget restrictions (Ministry of National Education, 2005). Turkish compulsory education is free in state schools for twelve years, including primary school to high school (p. 4). Individuals with special needs attended special education institutions and/or primary education institutions for their primary education with the Decree Law No. 573 on Special Education (*World Data on Education*, 2012).

The Ministry of National Education report identified that 84,580 students were enrolled in inclusive classrooms and 18,541 students were enrolled in special education classrooms at the primary level during the 2010–2011 school year (as cited in *World Data on Education*, 2012, p. 15). Turkey's education system is affected by multiple international organizations with which it has been involved. Turkey has been a member of the United Nations (UN) since the UN was founded in 1945 (*The United Nations Organization and Turkey*, n.d.).

Therefore, UN-based organizations such as the United Nations Educational, Scientific, and Cultural Organization (UNESCO) and the World Bank have had an impact on the Turkish education system. Furthermore, other international organizations, such as the Organization for Economic Cooperation and Development (OECD) and European Union (EU), are some of the organizations that have impacted Turkey's education system. Turkey developed projects to fulfill the needs of its education system.

For example, *Special Education Project (2004)* and *Special Education Empowering Project (2011–2013)* were some of the examples that are promoted by OECD (Organisation for Economic Cooperation and Development [OECD], 2013). Turkey has taken steps to reach the level of EU and OECD countries by improving the schooling rate and expanding pre-primary education to ensure that equality of opportunity is nationwide (Education, Audiovisual and Culture Executive Agency [EACEA], 2009/2010).

Special Education Program Attribute

The purpose of special education in Turkey is to provide the best educational opportunities for individuals with special needs by integrating them into the society to learn professional skills ("Ministry of National Education," 2005). Individuals who are eligible for special education services must meet the criteria of:

> (1) having mental deficiency, (2) having multiple deficiencies, (3) attention deficit hyperactivity disorder, (4) language and speech deficiency, (5) emotional and behavioral disorders, (6) visual impairment, (7) hearing impairment, (8) orthopedic impairment, (9) Autism, and (10) those identified as gifted. (EACEA, 2009/2010)

Individuals with special needs are ensured support in terms of flexibility of space, equipment, and programs in schools by attending the applied special education program together with typical children. They are prepared to develop their skills for living, vocational schools, or higher education according to individual needs and interests. The special education process for supportive education in Turkey begins with educational assessment and diagnosis of individuals determined by the authorized health institutions and approved by the Special Education Evaluation Boards (EACEA, 2009/2010).

Medical diagnosis of autism is made by the specialist at the hospital. Educational diagnosis for gifted children is made through an observation process by the center at the schools that those children are going to attend. Educational materials, instructional plans, special education programs, and the placements at an appropriate public school or at an institution will be provided for individuals with special needs in accordance with the special education assessment report (EACEA, 2009/2010).

Special Education Leadership Research Example

The study was conducted in eastern Turkey. There were fifty-one educators who performed leadership and administrative roles who participated in the study. Findings of this study indicated that participants' leadership style was a mixture of both transactional and transformational leadership skills (Gençer and Samur, 2016). In another study, principals and teachers noted that school principals demonstrated more transformational leadership style than transactional style (Sahin, 2004).

In one study, four school principals were interviewed about their leadership role. This study investigated the effects of the leadership roles of the principals at the special education schools concerning teacher perspective, school climate, and personnel involvement in decision making (Ustun, 2017). The research indicated that all principals have their own strategies and characteristics to provide more effective education (Ustun, 2017).

For example, principals in the study indicated that creating a peaceful and trustworthy environment, making motivating speeches on work discipline, and a passion for the job were some of the strategies and characteristics that principals used. One principal in the study noted that he or she organized programs to provide better services aimed at parents and students with disabilities. In addition, the school provided psychological support for the families about their children with disabilities (Ustun, 2017).

The study by Ustun (2017) found that the principals performed visionary, educational, and transformational leadership roles; however, they performed the visionary leadership roles the most and the transformational leadership roles the least. The study suggested it was essential for future educational leaders to "determine a vision for themselves and [reflect] this vision to the school climate" (p. 508).

Ustun (2017) further described that visionary leadership was a positive leadership feature that can increase the success of an institution. To achieve the purpose of increasing the school's success, the visionary leaders who work at special education institutions can improve themselves with new thoughts and actions to support teachers, students, and parents. It is important for school leaders who perform a visionary leadership role to convey their visions as they involve teachers' and parents' perspectives in their decisions in order to create a positive educational environment (Ustun, 2017).

Conclusion

The leaders of higher education institutions all over the world recognize the challenges of transforming themselves and address the increase in globalization (Foskett and Maringe, 2010). The paradigm shift of advancement of technology, global sharing, industrialization, and economic development is affecting national and global educational leadership cultures (Bissessar, 2018). However, a number of school personnel and practitioners have questioned the extent to which inclusion practices are performed in the school (Miškolci, Armstrong, and Spandagou, 2016).

A study in Poland by Dorczak (2011) indicated that the education system can be limited by education laws in the dominant bureaucratic culture. Contemporary schools need inclusive education leadership that can be developed within the particular organizational culture. Transformation is needed for the schools' organizational culture to develop a culture more supportive of inclusive leadership and inclusion. According to Mazurkiewicz (2011), inclusive educational leadership reform must focus on teacher training, including interpersonal and ethical aspects, and school self-evaluation.

According to Ward and colleagues (2015), three approaches to leadership have been implemented globally to enhance equity: critical reflection, the cultivation of a common vision of equity, and transforming dialogue. Head teachers have the power to voice and advocate for social justice. Moving forward, the study by Lyons (2016) showed that prospective principals require knowledge, skills, and dispositions to initiate and sustain their inclusive practices. Principal leadership is identified as a key to success in implementing inclusive education for students with disabilities.

In summary, reaching a consensus about practicing inclusion is not only about teaching and designing the curriculum but also about how education leaders practice their leadership in the school (Booth and Ainscow, 2011). School leaders play an important role in motivating teachers to build inclusive classrooms by promoting inclusive cultures, in-service training, enquiry, and evidence-based collaboration (Qeleni, 2013). The tasks of school leaders include providing intellectual stimulation and individual support and establishing positive working relationships with key stakeholders in order to promote school improvement and change (Bissessar, 2018).

References

Argyris, C., and Schön, D. (1974). *Theory in practice: Increasing professional effectiveness*. San Francisco, CA: Jossey-Bass.

Argyris, C., and Schön, D. (1978). *Organizational learning: A theory of action perspective*. Reading, MA: Addison-Wesley.

Bermani, M. I. (2017). *The extent to which principals' leadership and decision-making processes exerts influence on the operations of inclusion classrooms including students with autism spectrum disorder at the elementary school level* (Doctoral dissertation). Available from ProQuest Database (Accession No. 10674053).

Bissessar, C. (2018). An application of Hofstede's cultural dimension among female educational leaders. *Education Sciences*, 8(2), 77. doi-org.ezp.slu.edu/10.3390 /educsci8020077

Block, J. H. (2000). The odyssey of comprehensive school reform programs. In J. H. Block, S. T. Everson, and T. R. Guskey (Eds.), *Comprehensive school reform: A program perspective* (pp. 3–13). Dubuque, IA: Kendall/Hunt.

Bolman, L. G., and Deal, T. E. (2017). *Reframing organizations: Artistry, choice, and leadership* (sixth edition). Hoboken, NJ: John Wiley and Sons.

Booth, T., and Ainscow, M. (2011). *Index for inclusion: Developing learning and participation in schools*. Bristol, UK: Center for Studies on Inclusive Education.

Carter, S. L. (2006). The development of special education services in Thailand. *International Journal of Special Education*, 21(2), 32–36.

Cordeiro, P. A., and Cunningham, W. G. (2013). *Educational leadership: A bridge to improved practice*. Upper Saddle River, NJ: Pearson.

Cuban, L. (1987). *How teachers taught: Constancy and change in American classrooms 1880 to 1990*. New York, NY: Teachers College Press.

Deng, M. (2008). The attitudes of primary school teachers toward inclusive education in rural and urban China. *Frontiers of Education in China*, 3(4), 473–92.

Deng, M., and Jing, S. (2013). From learning in regular classrooms to equal regular education: Reflections on the locations of inclusive education in China. *Chinese Journal of Special Education*, 8(5), 3–9.

Deng, M., and Manset, G. (2000). Analysis of the "Learning in Regular Classrooms" movement in China. *Mental Retardation*, 38(2), 124–30. doi:10.1352/0047 -6765(2000)038<0124:AOTLIR>2.0.CO;2.

Dorczak, R. (2011). School organizational culture and inclusive educational leadership. *Contemporary Management Quarterly / Wspólczesne Zarządzanie*, 2, 45–55.

Education, Audiovisual and Culture Executive Agency. (2009/2010). *Organization of the education system in Turkey*. Retrieved from https://www.etf.europa.eu/sites/ default/files/m/60E61005D5CC5AD1C1257AA30025212F_Organization%20 of%20the%20education%20system%20in%20Turkey%202009.2010.pdf.

Everson, S. T. (2000). Selecting school improvement programs. In J. H Block, S. T. Everson, and T. R. Guskey (Eds.), *Comprehensive school reform: A program perspective* (pp. 379–95). Dubuque, IA: Kendall/Hunt.

Fang, J. (2009). *Inclusive education: The development of special education.* Retrieved from http://theory.people.com.cn/GB/10609681.html.

Foskett, N., and Maringe, F. (2010). *Globalization and internationalization in higher education: Theoretical, strategic and management perspectives.* London, England: Bloomsbury Academic.

Fry, G. W., and Bi, H. (2013). The evolution of educational reform in Thailand: The Thai educational paradox. *Journal of Educational Administration, 51*(1), 290–319. doi: 10.1108/09578231311311483.

Fry, G. W., Bovornsiri, V., and Uampuang, P. (1996). Cultural influences on higher education in Thailand. In K. M. Kempner and W. G. Tierney (Eds.), *Social role of higher education* (pp. 55–77). New York, NY: Garland.

Fulk, B. M., Swerdlik, P. A., and Kosuwan, K. (2002). Special education in Thailand. *Teaching Exceptional Children, 34*(5), 73. Retrieved from http://ezp.slu.edu/login?url=http://search.ebscohost.com/login.aspx?direct=true&db=eue&AN=507761204&site=eds-live.

Fullan, M. (2001). *Leading in a culture of change.* San Francisco, CA: Jossey-Bass.

Fullan, M., and Quinn, J. (2016). *Coherence.* Thousand Oaks, CA: Corwin.

Gençer, M. S., and Samur, Y. (2016). Leadership styles and technology: Leadership competency level of educational leaders. *Social and Behavioral Sciences, 229*, 226–33. doi:10.1016/j.sbspro.2016.07.132.

Grimes, P. (2013). Considering the continuing development of inclusive teachers: A case study from Bangkok, Thailand. *European Journal of Special Needs Education, 28*(2), 187–202. doi:10.1080/08856257.2013.778112.

Huang, Z. (2001). 试论全纳教育的价值取向 [On the orientation for value of inclusive education]. *Studies in Foreign Education, 28*(2), 17–22.

Huang, Z. (2004). *Inclusive education: Focus on learning and involvement among all the students.* Shanghai, China: Shanghai Education Press.

Huang, Z. (2014). 全纳教师教育:国外教师教育的新趋势 [Inclusive education: The new trend of teacher education in foreign countries]. *Journal of Teacher Education, 4*(5), 4–11.

Jiang, W., Wu, R., and Du, P. (2017). 全纳教育理念下传统教师教育的短板与改革路径 [Short board of traditional teachers' education under the concept of inclusive education and the reform part]. *Educational Review, 8*, 115–19.

Kantavong, P., Nethanomsak, T., and Luang-ungkool, N. (2012). Inclusive education in Thailand after 1999 National Education Act: A review of a pre-service teacher education system. *Procedia-Social and Behavioral Sciences, 69*, 1043–51.

Kantavong, P., and Sivabaedya, S. (2010). A professional learning program for enhancing the competency of students with special needs. *International Journal of Whole Schooling, 6*(1), 53. Retrieved from https://files.eric.ed.gov/fulltext/EJ872441.pdf.

Keenoy, P. (2012). *Principal preparation and support for special education* (Doctoral dissertation). Available from ProQuest LLC (ED547478).

Lei, X. (2015). 南非全纳教育的发展历史研究 [*The research of inclusive education historical development in South Africa*] (Unpublished master's thesis). Guangxi Normal University, Guangxi Province, China.

Leithwood, K. (2019). *Leadership development on a large scale: Lessons for long-term success*. Thousand Oaks, CA: Corwin.

Li, J. (2016). 加拿大全纳教育实践及启示 [The practice and enlightenment of inclusive education in Canada]. *The Guide of Science and Education*, 7, 5–7.

Liu, C., Du, X., and Yao, J., (2000). 普通小学教师对特殊儿童接纳态度的研究 [Study on primary school teachers' attitudes toward children with special needs to accept]. *Chinese Journal of Special Education*, 3, 34–36.

Lyons, W. (2016). Principal preservice education for leadership in inclusive schools. *Canadian Journal of Action Research*, 17(1), 36–50.

Marzano, R. J., Waters, T., and McNulty, B. A. (2005). *School leadership that works: From research to results*. Aurora, CO: McREL.

Mazurkiewicz, G. (2011). *Evaluation in pedagogical supervision: Reflections*. Kraków, Poland: Wydawnictwo.

Miles, M. B., Saxl, E. R., and Lieberman, A. (1988). What skills do educational "change agents" need? An empirical view. *Curriculum Inquiry*, 18(2), 157–93.

Ministry of Education, the Thai National Commission of the United Nations Educational, Scientific and Cultural Organization. (2015). *Education for all 2015 national review report: Thailand*. Retrieved from http://unesdoc.unesco.org/images/0022/002298/229878E.pdf.

Ministry of National Education—Republic of Turkey. (2005). *Basic education in Turkey: Background report*. Retrieved from http://www.oecd.org/education/school/39642601.pdf.

Miškolci, J., Armstrong, D., and Spandagou, I. (2016). Teachers' perceptions of the relationship between inclusive education and distributed leadership in two primary schools in Slovakia and New South Wales (Australia). *Journal of Teacher Education for Sustainability*, 18(2), 53–65.

Mu, G. M., Wang, Y., Wang, Z., Feng, Y., Deng, M., and Liang, S. (2015). An enquiry into the professional competence of inclusive education teachers in Beijing: Attitudes, knowledge, skills, and agency. *International Journal of Disability, Development and Education*, 62(6), 571–89.

Opartkiattikul, W., Arthur-Kelly, M., and Dempsey, I. (2014). From policy to practice: Supporting students with diverse needs in Thailand: Critical issues and implications. *International Journal of Whole Schooling*, 11(1), 1–18.

Organization for Economic Cooperation and Development. (2013). Education development for disabled and at-risk students in South-East Europe. Retrieved from http://www.oecd.org/education/innovation-education/35870597.pdf.

Peng, X. (1994). 美国全纳性教 [American inclusive education]. *Special Children and Teachers' Education*, 3, 33–38.

关于完善残疾儿童随班就读政策的提案 [Proposal for improving the policy of children with disabilities in regular classroom]. (2017). Retrieved from http://news.eastday.com/eastday/13news/auto/news/china/20170303/u7ai6559303.html.

Qeleni, M. T. (2013). *School leadership that motivates teachers to build inclusive classrooms* (Unpublished master's thesis). University of Oslo, Oslo, Norway.

Reeves, D. B. (2006). *The learning leader: How to focus school improvement for better results*. Alexandria, VA: The Association for Supervision and Curriculum Development.

Sahin, S. (2004). The relationship between transformational and transactional leadership styles of school principals and school culture: The case of Izmir, Turkey. *Educational Sciences: Theory and Practice, 4*(2), 387–95.

Sarason, S. B. (1996). Revisiting "the culture of the school and the problem of change." New York, NY: Teachers College Press.

Schulze, R. J. (2014). *School principal leadership and special education knowledge*. Retrieved from https://scholarworks.umass.edu/cgi/viewcontent.cgi?article=1016&context=dissertations.

Tangkitvanich, S., and Sasiwuttiwat, S. (2012). Revamping the Thai educational system: Quality for all. *TDRI Quality Review, 27*(2), 1–20. Retrieved from https://tdri.or.th/wp-content/uploads/2012/09/t5j2012.pdf.

The United Nation Organizations and Turkey. (n.d.). Retrieved from http://www.mfa.gov.tr/the-united-nations-organization-and-turkey.en.mfa.

Ustun, A. (2017). Effects of the leadership roles of administrators who work at special education schools upon organizational climate. *Universal Journal of Educational Research, 5*(3), 504–9.

Villa, R. A., and Thousand, J. S. (2003). Making inclusive education work. *Educational Leadership, 61*(2), 19–23.

Wang, B. (2012). 韩国全纳教育的发展、实施策略及面临问题 [The development, implementation strategy and problems of inclusive education in Korea]. *Chinese Journal of Special Education, 4*, 8–13.

Wang, J. (2002). *Inclusive education in UK: Implications for teaching reform in regular classes in China* (英国全纳教育研究--对我国随班就读教改实验的启示) (Unpublished master's thesis). Huadong Normal University, Shanghai, China.

Ward, S. C., Bagley, C., Lumby, J., Woods, P., Hamilton, T., and Roberts, A. (2015). School leadership for equity: Lessons from the literature. *International Journal of Inclusive Education, 19*(4), 333–46.

World Data on Education. (2012). Retrieved from http://www.ibe.unesco.org/fileadmin/user_upload/Publications/WDE/2010/pdf-versions/Turkey.pdf.

Xiao, F. (2005). 中国随班就读:历史•现状•展望 [Mainstreaming in China: History, actuality, perspectives]. *Chinese Journal of Special Education, 3*, 3–7.

Xiao, F. (2007). The Chinese "learning in a regular classroom": History, current situation, and prospects. *Chinese Education and Society, 40*(4), 8–20.

Xu, S. Q., Cooper, P., and Sin, K. (2018). The "Learning in Regular Classrooms" initiative for inclusive education in China. *International Journal of Inclusive Education, 22*(1), 54–73.

Xu, T., Sun, Y., and Lei, J. (2010). 澳大利亚全纳教育的发展及其启示 [The development and enlightenment of all-inclusive education in Australia]. *Studies in Foreign Education, 37*(1), 27–32.

Yell, M. L., Drasgow, E., and Lowrey, K. A. (2005). No child left behind and students with autism spectrum disorders. *Focus on Autism and Other Developmental Disabilities, 20*(3), 130–39. doi:10.1177/10883576050200030101.

Zhao, X. (2010). 美国全纳教育研究--历史、现状及启示 [*A study of inclusive education in the U.S.A.: History, present situation and enlightenment to China*] (Unpublished master's thesis). Huazhong Normal University, Hubei Province, China.

CHAPTER THREE

Educational Leadership in Latin America

Equipping Orphans and Vulnerable Children for Success Beyond the Institution

Calvin G. Roso

The number of orphans and vulnerable children (OVC) in the world was nearly 140 million in 2015 (UNICEF, 2017). Of this number, 8 to 10 million children and infants in the world live in orphanages (Ahern, 2013). Orphans leaving the institution consistently lack the skills and disposition to succeed in jobs and life outside the orphanage (Anghel, 2011; Takayanagi, 2010) and, therefore, often return to poverty, the streets, or prison (Mhongera and Lombard, 2016).

In June 2000, the researcher was one of several presenters at a Christian school conference in Bogota, Colombia. On the last day of the visit, the presenters were introduced to one of the translators, Jeanene, who was holding a week-old baby boy. Jeanene Thicke was the founder of Children's Vision International Incorporated (CVII), an orphanage rescuing children from an area in the city called the snake pit. The researcher and his group were then invited to tour CVII. This visit to CVII instilled within the researcher a strong desire to help orphans through education.

This initial trip to Latin America was the first of many international opportunities for the researcher. In the following years, numerous doors opened to travel to other countries visiting Christian schools, churches, and orphanages. Each of these trips was either professional (working with accreditation and/or professional development for K–12 schools and universities) or religious (leading teams of teenagers to serve local pastors and their communities). The researcher's Christian beliefs challenged him to help the less fortunate. These religious beliefs coincided with professional research in education that also advocated the need to help OVC.

Christian churches and schools outside the United States often have orphanages and/or work with OVC in their communities. The number of OVC in the world has risen dramatically in the past twenty to thirty years due to wars and epidemics (UNICEF, 2017). Multiple leadership approaches, some research based and some not, are used by schools and churches to educate these children and help them emotionally, socially, and spiritually with the hope that they will someday become healthy adults.

Context

A current concern is that a majority of OVC who live in orphanages often return to the streets as adults (Freidus, 2011; Prisiazhnaia, 2008; Takayanagi, 2010). In 2014, the researcher visited a former Soviet Union country, where he met Alex (pseudonym), who worked with orphans there. "Of the 120,000 children in [our nation's] orphanages, one-third probably will not find a family," Alex said. Although the government supplied orphans with apartments once they became adults, only 20 percent of them actually took these apartments. "The other 80 percent will either live on the streets or, more likely, end up in prison or dead," Alex said.

During an extended interview, Alex spoke of his concerns for orphans. "The problem with orphans in our country is their inability to socialize with others in 'real society,'" he said. Alex discussed the ineffectiveness of institutionalization to prepare these children for real life. He said that the institutionalization of children hindered them from becoming successful adults. "Life-long mentoring relationships is an effective alternative. . . . The only way to help the orphans is to close the orphanages," Alex said. While some advocate the entire abandonment of orphanages and the institutionalization of children, this is not yet possible in many countries.

Parameters of the Study

The purpose of this study was to analyze the perceptions of two leaders to see how their successful orphanages prepared children for transition into adulthood. This multiple-case study examined how orphanages in Colombia and Guatemala helped their children transition from institutionalization to adulthood. The research question that guided the study was: How does each orphanage prepare its children for success in life after the orphanage? An additional question considered was: What, if any, leadership styles or theories were evident in these orphanages?

The researcher examined institution documents (web-based and mailed newsletters) and solicited feedback from each orphanage leader through email-based interviews (Burns, 2010). Open-ended interview questions were developed based on the review of the literature in the area of transitional education for orphans. Email-based interviews were chosen in lieu of telephone or Skype conversations to help enrich the research (Burns, 2010). Email interviews were also effective in their flexibility to get feedback from people who otherwise might not be accessible (Kivits, 2005; O'Connor et al., 2008; Pattision, O'Gara, and Rattray, 2015).

The data from each institution were evaluated separately, and the interview findings were sent to each participant for member-checking to see what, if any, additions or corrections were necessary (Birt et al., 2016; Creswell, 2003). The findings of each institution were then analyzed to see any themes that emerged. The themes of each institution were then triangulated to see what, if any, common approaches the two orphanages had relating to transitional education.

This study was limited to an analysis of two orphanages in Latin America and what they did to help children effectively transition from institutionalization to adulthood. These orphanages were purposefully chosen by the researcher, who observed the institutions as being effective in meeting both the initial and long-term needs of the OVC they served. The early stages of this study considered that perhaps a leadership theory or style would emerge from the interviews. However, as the study progressed, it seemed that what helped the children succeed was larger than the individual leaders.

Literature

Ample research exists supporting the need for the care and education of OVC (Gjøtterud and Krogh, 2017; Levin and Hanes, 2007; Mhongera and Lombard, 2016; UNICEF, 2017, 2018). OVC education is unique because there are often significant cognitive, emotional, and social growth delays in OVC due to trauma and other issues (Aicha Briggs, 2012; Levin and Haines, 2007). In addition to caring for the social, emotional, and academic needs of OVC, some research is discovering the benefits of attending to children's spiritual needs (Fernando and Ferrari, 2011; Kosher and Asher, 2017).

One goal for OVC care and education is to generate resilience within students to help them later cope with the transition to adulthood (Anghel, 2011; Mhongera and Lombard, 2016; Prisiazhnaia, 2008). Some studies regarding effective transitional education for OVC suggest that positive outcomes of relationships and transformative education help OVC transition from childhood to adulthood (Batsche et al., 2014; Astoiants, 2007). The researcher examined studies regarding transitional education, relationships in orphanages, transformative learning, and applicable leadership theories.

Transitional Education
The difficulty of transitioning to adulthood is experienced by OVC (Deters and Bajaj, 2008; Emond, 2009; Freidus, 2011; Prisiazhnaia, 2008; Takayanagi, 2010) as well as foster children in the United States (Batsche et al., 2014; Dworsky, Napolitano, and Courtney, 2013; Morton, 2017). In one study, researchers (Prisiazhnaia, 2008) interviewed Russian adults raised in orphanages. Those interviewed said they struggled with dependence on the institution and feelings of pessimism regarding their futures. Other studies confirmed OVC need transitional care to cope with post-institution life (Mhongera and Lombard, 2016; Prisiazhnaia, 2008).

To help compensate for children's lack of social experience and to prepare them for life beyond the institution, one boarding school developed a "Social Life Orientation" course (Prisiazhnaia, 2008). Other OVC educators and schools advocate helping students form healthy attitudes toward the world (Pantiukhina, 2009), learn household responsibilities (Jacobi, 2009), practice apprenticeships (Jacobi, 2009), discuss morality (Deters and Bajaj, 2008), and analyze how to adapt to new situations (Prisiazhnaia, 2008). Education in social skills teaches healthy interaction and empathy for others (Kaler and Freeman, 1994; Shakhmanova, 2010).

Relationships in OVC Education
Positive relationships between OVC, adults, and other children promotes personal growth and future resilience (Deters and Baja, 2008; Friedus, 2011; Greener, 2003). Organizations create relationships between local communities and OVC (del Valle et al., 2011) to meet the relational needs of children. Healthy supportive relationships and the freedom to share one's feelings with others helps OVC succeed in the institution while giving them strength to transition to adulthood (Khoo, Mancinas, and Skoog, 2015). Institutions with a home atmosphere are also effective in building resilience for times of transition (Khoo, Mancinas, and Skoog, 2015).

Transformative Learning
Transformative learning (Mezirow, 1996) is an adult learning theory that views development into adulthood as a learning process, teaching students

external coping skills from reflective activities. Active participation in reflection activities is important for changing students' perspectives and influencing their coping skills in new contexts.

OVC and children of poverty must be equipped with new cultural values to succeed in life (Deters and Bajaj, 2008; Sánchez-Jankowski, 2008; Vaisey, 2010). Transformative learning is evident in OVC education (Gjøtterud and Krogh, 2017; Schvaneveldt and Spencer, 2016) as a method to strengthen post-institution resiliency in students' lives. Engaging students in activities that encourage them to see other perspectives helps them reflect on their own lives and future choices.

Relevant Leadership Theories
At the beginning of this study, the researcher assumed one particular leadership theory or style would emerge from the interviews to answer how each orphanage prepared its children for success in life after the orphanage. Theories that were initially considered applicable to effective orphan education were transformational leadership (Bass, 1985; Burns, 1978), servant leadership (Greenleaf, 1997), and total leadership (Schwahn and Spady, 1998, 2010). A review of the literature found that global transformational leadership (Lewis, Boston, and Peterson, 2017) should also be considered in the discussion of effective orphan education.

Transformational leaders (Bass, 1985; Burns, 1978) motivate their followers to participate by lifting group morale and encouraging moral development. The transformational leader also encourages participants to focus on service, efficiency, and producing a quality product (in schooling, this would mean producing a quality education). A transformational leader often uses charisma to move others past self-interests to consider the well-being of others.

Servant leaders (Greenleaf, 1997) are just as concerned about the well-being of their followers as they are about themselves and the goals of the organization. The servant leader leads by serving and is often seen working alongside his or her employees. A servant leader motivates through relationship and a focus on the well-being of his or her employees.

Total leaders (Schwahn and Spady, 1998, 2010) impact multiple areas in the organization by "defining purpose," "framing vision," "developing ownership," "building capacity," and "ensuring support" (Schwahn and Spady 1998, pp. 22–23). A total leader is future focused and is motivated by a cause that is greater than himself or herself.

Global transformational leaders (Lewis, Boston, and Peterson, 2017) are charismatic, visionary, motivational leaders who "are not only equipped with the traditional [transformational leadership] skills but also cross-cultural skills to navigate the murky waters of globalization" (p. 3). This leader is a critical thinker, influential in his or her society, is culturally sensitive, adaptable, and a person of high moral character. He or she makes decisions for the common good and creates an "environment that adopts and embraces change" (p. 5).

Findings

Children's Vision International

Mission

Children's Vision International Incorporated began in 1993 in Bogota, Colombia, after Jeanene Thicke-Sanderson, the head of CVII, found a three-month-old baby in the trash bitten by rats. "I called my parents and told them, 'I found a baby and I want her.' They said, 'Jeanene, do whatever it takes.'" Since its inception, CVII has expanded to include dental care, medical outreaches, and humanitarian aid, saving children from starvation, abuse, homelessness, and death squads. The mission of CVII is "to change the destiny of the destitute" (https://www.childrensvision.org).

Rescuing high-risk children in Bogota and surrounding impoverished communities, providing the children with food, a place to sleep, clothing, medical care, an education, and giving them "a place they can call home with people who love them" are all part of the ministry of CVII. "CVII's mission is to change lives through the living and written Gospel. We do not use the words 'orphanage,' 'orphan,' or 'abandon,'" said Thicke-Sanderson. "Once CVII begins to help, we become their family." CVII also works with the children's biological families whenever possible. Colombian regulations do not allow CVII to adopt out any children.

Demographics and Environment

Currently, CVII has four homes and is completing construction of an all-purpose building. They have a guest facility and a garage for children's workshops and are also constructing a multipurpose facility that will include a medical unit. One home serves babies and toddlers, and the other homes house boys and girls separately. "There is not a specific age cut-off, because we do not kick the children back onto the street once they turn eighteen," said Thicke-Sanderson. There are an additional one hundred students who do not live in the homes but do attend their school.

Each home is three or four floors tall and contains several small bedrooms, having four to six children in each room. Each home has its own recreational area, dining room, laundry, and bathrooms. The CVII properties are in a poor urban neighborhood in Bogota, Colombia, and do not include outside parks or recreational areas other than some small concrete play areas. They also lack opportunities for students to regularly experience life outside of the congested city.

CVII differs from government-sponsored Colombian orphanages in several ways. In most cases, government-sponsored orphanages do not offer their children family, affection, or further education. Thicke-Sanderson said,

> The biggest difference between government orphanages and us is that we believe in family. Family brings hope, and hope brings a future. For us poverty is not a sin, and children do not have to be abandoned [just] because they lack money. We try very hard to keep the family ties strong even when a parent is in prison or on the street doing drugs or prostitution. God can change a life, a family, and a destiny, if we give him a chance.

In government homes, students are kicked out when they turn eighteen years old, even if the children are not ready or able to support themselves. CVII, however, supports their young adults, equipping them with further education, counseling, and support as they transition into adulthood through their school, Beginning of Wisdom School.

Schooling and Curriculum

Beginning of Wisdom School was founded in 2002. The school name supports the Christian belief that the fear or respect of God is the beginning of wisdom (Psalm 111:10, Proverbs 1:7). The school mission is to teach students the importance of respecting God while also equipping them in academics (including English), social skills, and related activities. Classes are twenty students or less with all teachers certified by the Colombian Ministry of Education. In 2013, the school received accreditation for its technical college's electrical technician program.

Teachers and staff are trained through the Red Cross, the Colombian Health Department, and the National Police. Several of the teachers are also certified in special education. Teachers and staff also receive training from psychiatric clinics and universities to help children deal with ongoing anger management and anxiety issues due to trauma.

Children are also required to serve others in the community. CVII takes their children to the poorer communities in the nearby mountains to help distribute food and meet basic medical needs of the families. Approximately fifty children from these communities are given free scholarships to attend

Beginning of Wisdom School. CVII uses these outreaches as opportunities to teach their children to reflect on the importance of helping others.

Success

A number of children have completed technical programs at the school and were employed in the community. In addition, several of the children have attended universities in Colombia and in the United States. Five children are now police officers, some are missionaries, and others are married with children of their own.

According to Thicke-Sanderson, "To us, true success is that these children will grow up to be productive members of society who will never abandon their children. We want to see them achieve their dreams and become part of the answer to society, and no longer the problem."

Leadership

While founding CVII in an area that was initially opposed to helping street children, Thicke-Sanderson championed their needs in the midst of adversity. Her determination and cultural sensitivity influenced the community, local churches, and eventually the government. "When I found tiny children living in boxes under bridges, I could not walk away and say it didn't matter. I asked them their names. I fed them, and I became their friend" (Thicke-Sanderson, as cited in Hessel, 2009, p. 16). Her leadership convinced others to help build four children's homes, a school, and a clinic—impacting Bogota and the surrounding communities.

Casa Angelina

Mission

Casa Angelina was founded in 2003 in the Guatemalan mountains of Chimaltenango to help break the cycle of poverty in children's lives. All of the children at Casa Angelina are placed by the Guatemalan court system. "We treat the child's mental, physical, emotional, and social needs through the avenues God has given us and instructed us in," said Bethany Frazer, director of Casa Angelina. The orphanage was founded by and runs under the organization What Matters Ministries and Missions (WMMM), whose goal is "to build the local church, Feed the Poor, Rescue Orphans, Help Widows, and Win Souls Around the World" (whatmattersmm.org).

Bethany Frazer's parents, Ivan and Kimberly Tait, are the directors of WMMM, and they founded Casa Angelina in response to the misuse of funds they had seen in orphanages in several countries. The goal of Casa Angelina is to connect 1 million people with 1 million orphans.

> Children are not just provided for but are also rescued from a destructive path that would lead to the cycle of poverty, abuse, and brokenness continually repeating itself through the generations. Our goal is not to simply provide them with a safe place but to go beyond that and provide them with a fertile field to plant their dreams and, in many cases, to dream for the first time. (whatmattersmm.org)

Demographics and Environment

Over ninety children currently live at the orphanage. Casa Angelina is set up as smaller homes, each holding four staff members and up to fifteen children. The orphanage houses infants through young adults, and some children attend nearby colleges while living at Casa Angelina. Each home has wood-slatted ceilings, tile floors, leather couches, kitchens with long tables to seat the entire "family," and nice televisions. These nice amenities are intentional, showing the children that they are valued. "It's as if we are saying to them, 'You are worth the money we spent . . . and we want you to have the best,'" said Frazer. She noted,

> When new children come in, they are always met by a group of children who give them hugs and tell them they are going to be okay now. Our children, I believe, are some of our greatest helpers in restoring the lives of the new children that come. Children trust what other children tell them. And when they see so many happy, loving children who trust the adults they live with, that speaks volumes [to the new child].

Upon arrival, children are given a physical examination at the onsite clinic and then given their own clothing, shoes, toys, toiletries, and Bible. They are introduced to their new "home" and Casa Angelina family and shown their bed. This is usually the first bed many of the children have ever slept in. Children who are old enough are enrolled in Casa Angelina's private school. They are also counseled spiritually and emotionally by the onsite licensed child psychologist.

Casa Angelina is similar to other Guatemalan orphanages in that its children are appointed from the courts. Judges conduct follow-up hearings with children to ensure they are healthy and not being harmed. Very few children are adopted from the orphanage due to national adoption regulations.

Casa Angelina has a Christian emphasis, and pastors and workers care for each child's spiritual needs as well as his or her social, emotional, physical, and educational needs. To keep siblings together whenever possible, the orphanage accepts entire families (males and females), and although government orphanages force children to leave and find employment as early as age sixteen, Casa Angelina does not force children to leave at any particular age. Casa Angelina works to provide children with higher education to better equip them to be successful adults. Another difference at Casa Angelina is the individual homes and family environment. Frazer said,

> We have received children from state-run orphanages, and the staff of those orphanages often have abused and neglected the children. For example, one little boy we have grown up in a state orphanage from a baby to the age of five, and the staff who took care of him didn't even know his name. They [instead] referred to him by the color of his skin since he had a darker skin.

Schooling and Curriculum

The first emphasis at Casa Angelina is building children's well-being through relationships and understanding God's love for them and plan for their lives. Frazer said, "Many people comment on the thoroughness of the strategies and systems we have in place to care for the children and rehabilitate them mentally, physically, emotionally, and socially. We have a thorough 'all-around well-child' plan in place." This "plan" includes teaching children to cook and clean in their own "homes."

> We have found that continual repetition is very necessary. You have to be there to sow into their lives and help them remember "why" they are fighting for their futures, "why" they are worth it, and all that God has available for them. They need a ton of love and emotional support. We have found that the atmosphere of "family" here has meant so much to helping them feel stable and secure. It has also been a leading factor in their health in school outside of Casa Angelina, as they know that they have a family group to come home to and share their lives with.

Casa Angelina has a full-time private school for its children. Only qualified, licensed teachers are hired to teach, and the school is in compliance with government regulations. Frazer said, "We believe that our emphasis on higher education is a huge difference that sets us apart from other orphanages and that aids greatly in breaking the cycle of poverty in a child's life, preparing them well also for transition to adulthood."

Children fifteen years and older go through a specialized training program that includes Bible study, apologetics, leadership skills, and public speaking.

"We talk to them a lot about not having a victim or orphan mentality but to know God as their father and to find their own voices," said Frazer.

Children also learn environmental stewardship at Casa Angelina. The 16.5 acres of land include self-sustaining food production systems that link the facility's conventional aquaculture (fish production) with hydroponics (cultivating plants in water). There is also composting to enrich the soil for Casa Angelina's fruit trees and a system for water collection, purification, and storage.

Casa Angelina also teaches its children to give back through an outreach program. "When a child first comes, they feel broken and empty and they 'need' so much," said Frazer. "But after a while here, they get 'full,' and we notice their attitudes changing, and some start to demonstrate selfish tendencies." To help its children, Casa Angelina takes them to visit and adopt widows in the community.

> We visit them with our children and take them food, clean their little patch of earth, give them medical treatment, and love on them. We also adopt their families and grandchildren for Christmas and bring them presents and food that the children make. These outreaches have helped our children to realize that their hands are not full just for themselves, but that they always need to be pouring out and giving to others.

College-age children live in a "transition house" at Casa Angelina. Here they no longer live with adult workers but instead live with their peers and learn to take personal responsibility for household chores, time management, and so on. The transition house is intentional as a method for teaching children life lessons before they finish college and move away as adults.

Success

Success at Casa Angelina is measured by the changes in the children themselves. Children are graduating from the school and continuing their educations in colleges outside of Casa Angelina. While in college, they are adapting well with other young adults and building relationships outside of the orphanage. Monica, one of the children attending college while at Casa Angelina, said this about her experience:

> You create a healthy home environment for us to learn what a real family is and how it acts. You are different in the way you love us all. We learn how to have respect for the opinions of others in the way you respect us and teaching us to have our own voice and express ourselves. The atmosphere here makes us feel very comfortable. We feel at peace. And we feel loved, because in other

orphanages we feel afraid because we don't know what's going to happen and what type of people are there. But here we feel comfortable and know that we are safe.

You prepare us to be adults by giving us the examples of the staff who work here. Like Papa Ivan always says, "We have to do something with our lives so that we can help other people in the future." You teach us to always think about other people and not only ourselves and to help them in what we do.

Leadership

Frazer's highly relational leadership style is evident in the group homes for children. "We really do relationships well and have good success instilling purpose and motivation into the children to dream and pursue those dreams," said Frazer. Her emphasis on building a self-sustaining organization and transitional houses shows her keen awareness of cultural needs. Like Thicke-Sanderson, Frazer is a visionary, mission-driven leader who is constantly moving toward future steps while also remaining connected to the physical, academic, cultural, social, and spiritual needs of the children she serves.

Discussion and Recommendations

The purpose of this study was to analyze how the orphanages prepared children for transition into adulthood. The study of CVII and Casa Angelina revealed common themes regarding how successful orphanages prepare children for transition into adulthood. Both institutions have grown and progressed to better equip children for transitioning into adulthood.

The common methods among the two institutions included a Christian mission to serve children, family atmosphere, transformative learning, and service learning. While most of the findings of this study are supported by previous research, CVII and Casa Angelina have some unique components that might be helpful to other institutions caring for OVC. The findings of the study might be transferable to similar institutions or settings in other countries.

Christian Mission

Some research has shown that a spiritual emphasis in the institution helps build resilience in OVC (Fernando and Ferrari, 2011; Kosher and Asher, 2017). Both CVII and Casa Angelina are motivated to serve underprivileged children based on a Christian mission to help the orphan. This Christian mission was integrated throughout each institution's foundational and promotional materials as well as its curriculum and instruction.

Family Atmosphere

Many orphanages promote community participation, connections with family, and a home environment within the orphanage as a means of helping children cope and develop (Rus et al., 2010). Interactions with peers and adults is healthy and necessary for helping OVC develop (Astoiants, 2007; Khoo et al., 2015; Ogina, 2010; Strolin-Goltzman et al., 2016). Casa Angelina also promotes a family atmosphere by having students live in smaller homes for children and staff.

Transformative Learning

Research advocates that children of trauma need specific training to help them both manage past pain and cope with future uncertainties (Deters and Bajaj, 2008; Sánchez-Jankowski, 2008; Vaisey, 2010). The transformative learning approach is used in OVC education as a means of helping children process past experiences and create new life perspectives (Gjøtterud and Krogh, 2017; Schvaneveldt and Spencer, 2016).

Both orphanages trained students to see themselves and their futures as different from past experiences. CVII no longer called the children "orphans." "We do not use the words 'orphanage,' 'orphan,' or 'abandoned.' Once CVII begins to help, we become their family," said Thicke-Sanderson. "When our children go to school outside of Casa Angelina," said Frazer, "we want them to know they don't have to fit into a social class—upper or middle, family, or orphan. We want them to feel like they are enough in who they are and who God has created them to be. This is something we are continuing to work on."

Community Service and Service Learning

In addition to improving a sense of self-efficacy (Dahan, 2016) and personal identity (Eyler et al., 2001), service learning (SL) has proven effective in improving students' moral development and social values (Dahan, 2016) and the ability to work well with others (Farmer, Perry, and Ha, 2016), by looking beyond their own circumstances and gaining empathy for others (Toncar et al., 2006). Service learning also helps students apply their knowledge to the real world while building caring relationships.

Little previous research exists on the benefits of SL as a means of helping OVC grow in these areas. Both CVII and Casa Angelina used community service and SL experiences for their children. Each organization wanted their children to see that there is always someone who has it worse and to learn gratitude for their own experiences.

Leadership Styles
Jeanene Thicke-Sanderson and Bethany Frazer both exhibit characteristics common to those of global transformational leaders (Lewis, Boston, and Peterson, 2017). Transformational leadership skills (e.g., motivation, encouragement, focus on moral development) plus cultural awareness in a global context helps each of them to lead their organizations. A steadfast adherence to mission helped sustain both leaders during the early years of their organizations. Thicke-Sanderson was motivated by a mission to change the destiny of the children. Similarly, Frazer was motivated to break the cycles of poverty and abuse in the children she served.

Both leaders connect their mission to their view of God's love for children. The moral development of children is another similarity in both styles of leadership. "God can change a life, a family, and a destiny if we give him a chance," said Thicke-Sanderson. While their transformational leadership skills equipped them to establish their organizations, perhaps it is their global leadership and connection to the needs of the culture that helped them to sustain the organizations. Both leaders transformed their communities with an awareness of children's needs and a desire to do good.

Conclusion

Both orphanages and their corresponding schools were innovative in their approaches to educating their children and preparing them for successful transition into adulthood. Both Thicke-Sanderson from CVII and Frazer from Casa Angelina were effective global transformational leaders who were willingly flexible in their approaches to educate the children under their care. A "whatever it takes" attitude was common in both leaders and throughout the history of both institutions.

CVII and Casa Angelina each continue to learn and try new approaches to help their children achieve success beyond the orphanage. The Christian mission, family atmosphere, transformative learning, and SL used at these institutions are very effective in meeting the current and future needs of OVC. Schools, organizations, communities, and individuals helping OVC can learn from several of the approaches used by CVII and Casa Angelina to aid these children as they transition to adulthood.

References

Ahern, L. (2013, August 10). Orphanages are no place for children. *Washington Post*, p. 9.
Aicha Briggs, L. E. (2012). *What does it mean to care and provide schooling for a child orphaned due to HIV/AIDS in Côte d'Ivoire? A qualitative study* (Unpublished doctoral dissertation). University of Maryland, College Park, MD.
Anghel, R. (2011). Transition within transition: How young people learn to leave behind institutional care whilst their careers are stuck in neutral. *Children and Youth Services Review, 33*(12), 2526–31. doi:10.1016/j.childyouth.2011.08.013.
Astoiants, M. S. (2007). Orphaned children: An analysis of life and practices in a residential institution: An experiment in participant observation. *Russian Education and Society, 49*(4), 23–42. doi:10.2753/RES1060-9393490402.
Bass, B. M. (1999). Two decades of research and development in transformational leadership. *European Journal of Work and Organizational Psychology, 8*(1), 9–32.
Batsche, C., Hart, S., Ort, R., Armstrong, M., Strozier, A., and Hummer, V. (2014). Post-secondary transitions of youth emancipated from foster care. *Child and Family Social Work, 19*(2), 174–84.
Birt, L., Scott, S., Cavers, D., Campbell, C., and Walter, F. (2016). Member checking: A tool to enhance trustworthiness or merely a nod to validation? *Qualitative Health Research, 26*(13), 1802–11. doi:10.1177/1049732316654870.
Burns, E. (2010, November). Developing email interview practices in qualitative research. *Sociological Research Online, 15*(4), 8. Retrieved from http://www.socresonline.org.uk/15/4/8.html.
Burns, J. M. (1978). *Leadership: Transformational leadership, transactional leadership*. New York, NY: Harper and Row.
Creswell, J. W. (2003). *Research design: Qualitative, quantitative, and mixed methods approaches* (second edition). Thousand Oaks, CA: Sage.
Dahan, T. A. (2016). Revisiting pedagogical variations in service-learning and student outcomes. *International Journal of Research on Service-Learning and Community Engagement, 4*(1), 3–15.
del Valle, J. F., Lázaro-Visa, S., López, M., and Bravo, A. (2011). Leaving family care: Transitions to adulthood from kinship care. *Children and Youth Services Review, 33*(12), 2475–81.
Deters, L., and Bajaj, M. (2008). Orphans and vulnerable children in Ghana. A contextual analysis: ECCD stakeholders adapting the safety net. Master of Arts in International Educational Development at Teachers College, Columbia University, 1–21.
Dworsky, A., Napolitano, L., and Courtney, M. (2013). Homelessness during the transition from foster care to adulthood. *American Journal of Public Health, 103*(S2), S318–23.

Emond, R. (2009). I am all about the future world: Cambodian children's views on their status as orphans. *Children and Society*, 23, 407–17. doi:10.1111/j.1009-0860.2008.00189.x.

Eyler, J., Giles Jr., D. E., Stenson, C. M., and Gray, C. J. (2001). At a glance: What we know about the effects of service-learning on college students, faculty, institutions and communities, 1993–2000. *Higher Education*, 20(3), 1–120.

Farmer, B., Perry, L. G., III, and Ha, I. (2016). University-community engagement and public relations education: A replication and extension of service-learning assessment in the public relations campaigns course. *International Journal of Research on Service-Learning and Community Engagement*, 4(1), 235–54. Retrieved from http://journals.sfu.ca/iarslce.

Fernando, C., and Ferrari, M. (2011). Spirituality and resilience in children of war in Sri Lanka. *Journal of Spirituality in Mental Health*, 1(1), 52–77. doi:10.1080/19349637.2011.547138.

Freidus, A. L. (2011). *Raising Malawi's children: AIDS orphans and a politics of compassion* (Order No. 3468520). Available from ProQuest Dissertations and Theses Global (888043547). Retrieved from http://0search.proquest.com.patris.apu.edu/docview/888043547?accountid=8459.

Gjøtterud, S., and Krogh, E. (2017). The power of belonging. *International Journal for Transformative Research*, 4(1), 7–17.

Greener, S. (2003). Factors that optimize development. In G. Miles and J. J. Wright (Eds.), *Celebrating children: Equipping people working with children and young people living in difficult circumstances around the world* (pp. 40–47). Waynesboro, GA: Paternoster Press.

Greenleaf, R. K. (1997). *The servant as leader*. New York, NY: Paulist Press.

Hessel, S. T. (2009). Help travels around the world. *Coulee Region Women Magazine*. Retrieved from http://www.crwmagazine.com/pdf/archive/crw-dec-jan2009.pdf.

Jacobi, J. (2009, February–April). Between charity and education: Orphans and orphanages in early modern times. *Paedagogica Historica*, 45(1–2), 51–66.

Kaler, S. R., and Freeman, B. J. (1994). Analysis of environmental deprivation: Cognitive and social development in Romanian orphans. *Journal of Child Psychology and Psychiatry*, 35(4), 769–81.

Kivits, J. (2005). Online interviewing and the research relationship. In C. Hine (Ed.), *Virtual methods: Issues in social research on the Internet* (pp. 35–49). Oxford, England: Berg.

Khoo, E., Mancinas, S., and Skoog, V. (2015). We are not orphans. Children's experience of everyday life in institutional care in Mexico. *Children and Youth Services Review*, 59, 1–9.

Kosher, H., and Asher, B. (2017). Religion and subjective well-being among children: A comparison of six religion groups. *Children and Youth Services Review*, 80, 63–77.

Levin, K., and Haines, S. (2007, July). Opportunities for the development of communicative competence for children in an orphanage in South Africa. *Child Care in Practice, 13*(3), 221–36. doi:10.1080/13575270701353564.
Lewis, E., Boston, D., and Peterson, S. (2017). A global perspective of transformational leadership and organizational development. *Journal of Research Initiatives, 2*(3), 1–6.
Mezirow, J. (1996). Contemporary paradigms of learning. *Adult Education Quarterly, 46*(3), 158–72.
Mhongera, P. B., and Lombard, A. (2016). Poverty to more poverty: An evaluation of transition services provided to adolescent girls from two institutions in Zimbabwe. *Children and Youth Services Review, 64*(C), 145–54.
Morton, B. M. (2017). Growing up fast: Implications for foster youth when independence and early adulthood collide. *Children and Youth Services Review, 82*, 156–61. doi:10.1016/j.childyouth.2017.09.028.
O'Connor, H., Madge, C., Shaw, R., and Wellens, J. (2008). Internet-based interviewing. In N. Fielding, R. M. Lee, and G. Blank (Eds.), *The SAGE handbook of online research Methods* (pp. 271–89). London, England: Routledge.
Ogina, T. A. (2010). Teachers' pastoral role in response to the needs of orphaned learners. *International Journal of Education Policy and Leadership, 5*(12). Retrieved from http://www.ijepl.org.
Pattision, N., O'Gara, G., and Rattray, J. (2015, March 4). After critical care: Patient support after critical care. A mixed method longitudinal study using email interviews and questionnaires. *Intensive Critical Care Nursing, 31*(4), 213–22. doi:10.1016/j.iccn.2014.12.002.
Pantiukhina, E. N. (2009, September). The social and pedagogical protection of orphans in Russia. *Russian Education and Society, 51*(9), 40–59.
Prisiazhnaia, N. V. (2008, December). Orphan children: Adjusting to life after the boarding institution. *Russian Education and Society, 50*(12), 23–39. doi:10.2753/RES1060-9393501202.
Rus, A., Parris, S. R., Cross, D. R., and Purvis, K. B. (2010). Romanian institutionalized children's privation and Bronfenbrenner's Ecological System Theory. In *Research, Education and Development: Symposium Proceedings*. Cluj-Napoca: Risoprint Publishing House. doi:10.13140/2.1.5000.8004.
Sánchez-Jankowski, M. (2008). *Cracks in the pavement: Social change and resilience in poor neighborhoods.* Berkeley, CA: University of California Press.
Schvaneveldt, P., and Spencer, T. (2016). Impact of international humanitarian service-learning on emerging adult social competence: A mixed-methods evaluation. *Gateways: International Journal of Community Research and Engagement, 9*(1), 113–31.
Schwahn, C. J., and Spady, W. G. (1998). *Total leaders: Applying the best future-focused change strategies to education.* Arlington, VA: AASA.
Schwahn, C. J., and Spady, W. G. (2010). *Total leaders 2.0: Leading in the age of empowerment.* New York, NY: R&L Education.

Shakhmanova, A. S. (2010, May). Social and pedagogical problems of the upbringing of orphans in Russia. *Russian Education and Society, 52*(5), 71–78. doi:10.2753/RES1060-9393520506.

Strolin-Goltzman, J., Woodhous, V., Suter, J., and Werrback, M. (2016). A mixed method study on educational well-being and resilience among youth in foster care. *Children and Youth Services Review, 70*, 30–36.

Takayanagi, T. (2010). Orphans and vulnerable children's views to education in an urban slum of Zambia. In S. Howard (Ed.), *Australian Association for Research in Education. International Education Research conference proceedings*, Melbourne, 28 November–2 December 2010.

Toncar, M. F., Reid, J. S., Burns, D. J., Anderson, C. E., and Nguyen, H. P. (2006). Uniform assessment of the benefits of service learning: The development, evaluation, and implementation of the SELEB scale. *The Journal of Marketing Theory and Practice, 14*(3), 223–38.

UNICEF. (2017, June 16). Current issues: Orphans. Retrieved from https://www.unicef.org/media/media_45279.html.

UNICEF. (2018). Statistical tables. *State of the World's Children*, 146–205. Retrieved from https://read.un-ilibrary.org/children-and-youth/the-state-of-the-world-s-children-2017.

Vaisey, S. (2010). What people want: Rethinking poverty, culture, and educational attainment. *The Annals of the American Academy of Political and Social Science, 629*(1), 75–101.

CHAPTER FOUR

Notre Dame Mission Volunteers–AmeriCorps—A National Program with Significant Local Impact

Peter R. Litchka

Since 2012, the author of this chapter has completed three independent evaluations of the Notre Dame Mission Volunteers–AmeriCorps (ND-MVA), an educational support program found throughout the United States. These evaluations occurred in 2012, 2015, and 2018 and are required by all programs funded by AmeriCorps. This chapter is an examination and analysis of each of the three evaluations and a synthesis of the findings from the three evaluations.

Framework

Leadership in education continues to be a focus of scholars, policy makers, and practitioners, particularly as to how a school leader can have a positive impact on teaching and learning, and to what extent. According to Northouse,

> Despite the multitude of ways in which leadership has been conceptualized, the following components can be identified as central to the phenomenon: (a) leadership is a process, (b) leadership involves influence, (c) leadership occurs in groups, and (d) leadership involves common goals. Leadership is a process whereby an individual influences a group of individuals to achieve a common goal. (2016, p. 6)

It is anticipated that the reader will see how a commitment to three specific constructs of effective leadership described below can provide demonstrably enhanced program effectiveness, which ultimately enhances the educational opportunities for those young people who are often relegated to the margins:

- Leadership for social justice: an understanding of and a commitment by school leaders to creating and sustaining schools that focus on the processes, behaviors, and outcomes in support of all learners within the school, including those of different racial, gender, cultural, disability, sexual orientation, and socioeconomic groups (Allen, 2006; Evans, 2007; Jean-Marie, 2008).
- Servant leadership: leadership that focuses on the leader being cognizant and mindful of the needs, wants, and concerns of those being led; the leader's priority is to put followers first, to empower and enable them to be successful, and to ensure that each reaches his or her full potential. According to Greenleaf (1970), "the best test of servant leadership is: do those served grow as persons, do they, while being served, become healthier, wiser, freer, more autonomous, more likely themselves to become servant leaders? And, what is the effect on the least privileged in society; will they benefit, or, at least, will they not be further deprived?" (p. 15).
- Volunteerism: activity that is completely of one's free will, with no expected material rewards, done with complete strangers and/or specific beneficiaries over a long period of time (Haski-Leventhal, 2009; Penner, 2002).

Notre Dame Mission Volunteers–AmeriCorps

Notre Dame Mission Volunteers was founded in 1992 by the Sisters of Notre Dame de Namur to promote literacy in education by placing volunteers[1] in communities within the United States and around the world. Notre Dame Mission Volunteers believes that education is the central tool in the struggle of the poor for human dignity, self-esteem, and willpower.

"Notre Dame–AmeriCorps believes that education is fundamental in the struggle of the poor for human dignity, self-esteem, and self-determination. We seek to build community among our members, as well as the people with whom we work by reaching out across culture and class" (NDMVA, 2017).

NDMVA received its first grant from AmeriCorps in 1995. During the 2017–2018 school year, NDMVA had programs in twenty-seven cities across the United States that included almost 150 partnering sites, more than 375 members, and approximately 12,500 students being served. In addition, ND-

MVA supports four multicity, faith-based partnerships, including sixty-two sites serving more than nine hundred students.

The national office of NDMVA is located in Baltimore, Maryland, and includes an executive director and support staff to oversee, coordinate, lead, and manage the national network.

Within the individual program sites, a site director oversees the services being provided, coordinates with partnering sites where individual members serve, and is the primary liaison between the national office in Baltimore and the various partnering sites. Partnering sites include public schools, charter schools, private religious schools, and other community agencies in economically disadvantaged communities.

NDMVA teams serve with local partners to expand student access to quality educational programs, which include but are not limited to offering small-group and one-on-one instruction, both during and after school. Notre Dame–AmeriCorps members serve full time for eleven months, and during this time members receive training in the form of biweekly team meetings, a training conference in Maryland, and opportunities for additional training and retreats. Members are based at operating sites around the country, being assigned to local partnering sites that include schools as well as community and faith-based organizations.

Of note are the Nativity Affiliates, which are in several cities across the United States (Baltimore, Greater Boston, Hartford, St. Petersburg, and Tampa). Nativity Schools, which began in the early 1970s, are small middle schools found primarily in urban settings. These schools provide services to low-income students who may be at risk of eventually dropping out of school. The schools have an emphasis on a small student-to-teacher ratio. In addition, extended academic attention, including evening and weekend support, extra tutoring after school, and increasing parental involvement, are just some of the services provided. Regional site directors of the Nativity Affiliates oversee this part of the NDMVA program, reporting directly to the NDMVA executive director.

AmeriCorps

AmeriCorps, which is administered by the Corporation for National and Community Service (CNCS), provides grants to both public and nonprofit organizations that support community service at the local, state, and national level. The primary goals for AmeriCorps are to:

- *Satisfy Unmet Social Needs*—to help communities solve human social and economic problems
- *Develop Corps Members*—to provide opportunities for members to develop character and job preparation in terms of learning and experiences
- *Enhance Civic Ethics*—to create opportunities for members to develop civic consciousness as they help to build (rebuild) communities and develop partnerships as well. (CNCS, n.d.)

AmeriCorps's programs both enhance the communities in which they serve and create experiential learning opportunities for young adults who are preparing to enter the workforce. AmeriCorps has placed thousands of such young adults into positions in which they learn about service and apply such skills to local communities around the country (CNCS, n.d.).

Full-time AmeriCorps members complete up to 1,700 hours of service during a year and receive a living stipend, health benefits, and a residence to share with fellow members to assist in helping the elderly, the disabled, and students in schools. They often also work in conjunction with nonprofits such as Habitat for Humanity, Boys and Girls Clubs, the American Red Cross, and numerous faith-based and community initiatives. Since 1994, almost 1 million AmeriCorps members have provided more than 1 billion hours in service across the United States, taking on the various social and economic problems found in communities across the nation (CNCS, n.d.).

Program Evaluation Framework Overview

Evaluating a program is a mechanism for improving overall performance of a program, as it not only provides an opportunity to analyze effectiveness and efficiency but also allows for the organization that is managing the program to monitor and adjust strategies, test interventions, and use data to support the overall mission of the program. Simply put, program evaluation offers an organization the opportunity to study, appraise, and improve a particular program.

Effective program evaluation can have a significant impact on organizational problem solving, decision making, resource management, and communication based on the appropriate collection and use of empirical data from the evaluation. Rossi, Freeman, and Lipsey (2003) suggest that "program evaluation is the use of social research procedures to systematically investigate the effectiveness of social intervention programs" (p .4). According to Maxfield and Babbie (2008), program evaluation "refers to a research purpose rather than a specific research method" (p. 255).

There are numerous categories of program evaluations, with the following being the most common and general in nature:

- Formative evaluation: a type of evaluation that is conducted when a program is being developed or adapted; this type of evaluation makes certain that a program is feasible, appropriate, and acceptable *before* it is implemented.
- Process/implementation evaluation: a type of evaluation that determines whether or not the strategies and activities have been implemented as intended.
- Outcome/effectiveness evaluation: a type of evaluation that measures the impact on the target population in terms of assessing the progress in outcomes that the program is to achieve.
- Impact evaluation: more summative in nature, this type of evaluation assesses the effectiveness in whether or not the program achieved its ultimate goals. (Center for Disease Control and Prevention, 2018)

The evaluations being examined in this chapter are considered to be impact evaluations, described above. Evaluators can use quantitative, qualitative, or a mixed-methods approach for the collection of data and the subsequent analysis. It was agreed on by the evaluator, NDMVA, and AmeriCorps that a mixed-methods approach would be appropriate.

For the quantitative portion of the evaluation, surveys were used. More specifically, a survey was given to students early in the school year (thus described as a "pre-survey"), followed by the same survey given to students in May of the same school year (thus described as a "post-survey").

For the qualitative portion of the evaluation, focus groups and interviews were used to allow the evaluator to examine and understand how students, members, and teachers made meaning of the services that were provided by NDMVA as well as a means to confirm the data collected from the surveys.

Evaluations: 2012, 2105, and 2018

While each of the three evaluations focused on different evaluation questions and different NDMVA sites, there were two common features found among the three evaluations.

First, for quantitative measurements, surveys were used to measure pre- and post-differences in student perceptions related to improved academic achievement; attitudes toward learning, peers, and teachers; as well as differences in such perceptions between those receiving services, identified as the treatment group, and those receiving none of the services, identified as the control group. Surveys were administered in September and May of the particular evaluation year via Survey Monkey, an online survey platform.

Second, for qualitative measurements, interviews and focus groups occurred with randomly selected students as well as selected members and teachers. The semistructured nature of these interviews and focus groups focused on the following:

- Types of services students received
- Benefits of such services to students
- Challenges that students faced regarding services
- Overall impact of services on students, the school, and community

Each of the three evaluations was examined within the following five areas: context, survey instrument, focus and interviews, quantitative results, and qualitative results, with an overall discussion of the three evaluations presented in the final part of this chapter.

The 2012 Evaluation

The purpose of the program evaluation in 2012 was to assess the impact of the NDMVA in two areas: student attitudes and student achievement. In particular, this evaluation focused on the question of whether or not students receiving NDMVA services had a change in their attitudes toward learning over the course of the school year and to what extent was there a relationship between such change in attitudes and overall achievement.

Survey Instrument

The evaluator developed the survey using the theoretical construct that student learning and achievement is augmented when students have or develop positive attitudes toward learning, including but not limited to their own personal perceptions, their relationships to fellow students and teachers, as well as other school variables (Appleton, Christenson, and Furlong, 2008; Libbey, 2004).

There were four domains within the survey: perceptions of self-efficacy, perceptions of teachers, perceptions of other students, and the overall school climate. Surveys were designed for elementary and secondary students, with appropriate reading levels for both groups. Also, surveys were translated into Spanish. Demographic data were also collected, including student gender, ethnicity, and type of program the student was involved in. To be able to match students' responses from September to May, each student was given a unique identification number that included the first four letters of his or her name, his or her birthday, and the program name. For the October survey, 2,520 elementary students and 2,075 secondary students completed the survey. In May, 1,752 elementary students and 1,551 secondary students completed the survey.

Focus Groups and Interviews

The evaluator also completed a series of interviews with students and staff during the time period of February–April 2013. The evaluator visited four program cities, visiting a total of seventeen sites, interviewing seventy-nine students, fourteen NDMVA members, and nine teachers from participating schools. Interviews were recorded and later transcribed for analysis purposes.

To measure student achievement, student data were collected at each site in collaboration with local schools. Students met the level of success if they passed their English and/or math courses and/or were promoted to the next grade. Data were collected in June 2013. A total of 1,514 elementary and secondary students (64.7%) were matched to their participation in surveys with final grades/promotion.

Quantitative Results

A series of statistical analyses of the surveys, interviews, and student achievement success were completed. As shown in table 1, statistically significant and positive changes were found among elementary students between the October and May surveys in each of the four domains. Analysis of variance (ANOVA) was used to determine if the changes between the fall and spring surveys were significant among the various demographic groups, including gender, ethnicity, and type of service being received. Positive and statistically significant changes in student attitudes were found in both females and males, among the six ethnic groups, and according to the type of service being received.

Similar evidence was found with secondary students, as shown in table 2. Positive changes in attitudes were found in each of the four domains, including statistical significance in three of the four areas. Once again, ANOVA was then used to determine if the changes between the fall and spring surveys were significant among the various demographic groups found in the study, including gender, ethnicity, and type of service being received. Such analyses found statistically significant changes in both genders, three of the ethnic groups of secondary students (African Americans, Asian Americans, and Caucasians), and those students receiving in-school services.

Table 1. 2012 Evaluation: Paired Sample T-Test Fall Survey and Spring Survey Elementary Students (N=1,744)

Domains: Student Attitudes	Mean (SD)		Difference	Sig. (2-tailed) *
	Fall Survey	Spring Survey		
Self-Efficacy	2.25 (.48)	2.27 (.48)	.02	.011*
Toward Teachers	2.82 (.42)	2.98 (.45)	.16	.009*
Toward Fellow Students	2.39 (.46)	2.41 (.46)	.02	.012*
School Climate	2.59 (.46)	2.62 (.46)	.03	.014*
Total	10.05 (1.49)	10.29 (1.53)	.24	.013*

*=p<.05

Table 2. 2012 Evaluation: Paired Sample T-Test Fall Survey and Spring Survey Secondary Students (N=1,710)

Domains: Student Attitudes	Mean (SD)		Difference	Sig. (2-tailed) *
	Fall Survey	Spring Survey		
Self-Efficacy	3.43 (.46)	3.49 (.69)	.26	.017*
Toward Teachers	3.83 (.49)	3.90 (.75)	.07	.008*
Toward Fellow Students	3.87 (.60)	3.89 (.84)	.02	.273
School Climate	3.22 (.43)	3.35 (.66)	.13	.011*
Total	14.35 (1.38)	14.95 (1.43)	.24	.000*

*=p<.05

Qualitative Results

Both elementary and secondary students were interviewed as part of the qualitative portion of the evaluation. All interviews took place at the site where the program was being offered, mostly in schools but a limited number in nonschool settings.

A total of 173 comments were recorded from the interviews of thirty-seven elementary students. Regarding the types of services offered, help with schoolwork and help with homework received the most responses, followed by mentoring and enrichment services.

In terms of program benefits, becoming a better student and having adult support were the most numerous responses provided by the elementary students, followed by help with problems, feeling safe, and having a brighter future. A third-grade female student commented, "I do much better in school now than before. I feel as if I can do the work because not only does my teacher help me, but the teacher assistant [NDVMA member] is there with me all of the time. She helps when I am with all of the students and gives me help when I am by myself as well."

Two fourth-grade male students shared the following regarding the role of the mentors as role models who work in their school: "Juan [pseudonym] went to the same school we are now going to. He went to college and came back here to help, just like he told us that someone did that for him as well. He tells us that we at the school are a family who will always be there to help us. And we want to be just like him . . . get good grades and come back to help others."

Elementary students listed spending too much time on schoolwork as their biggest concern, followed by not having enough "fun" activities, not enough time, and other students not behaving. Finally, if the program ceased to exist, elementary students felt they would not be successful in school, would miss the mentors and adults from the program, and would not feel as safe or as happy. For example, one fifth-grade male student stated, "I finish school, then go upstairs for the after-school program. And we have to do our homework first, then we get a snack, then go to the gym. I just wish we could go outside first or go to the computer lab first, then eat, then do our homework. Some days, it feels like school all day until 5:30 at night."

The same student and his sister in fourth grade also commented that while they feel that there is so much schoolwork during the day and after school as well that they would not really want to be anywhere else: "We feel very safe here. My mother does not get home until 6:00, and we know other students go home to empty homes. We feel safe here, and we know our teachers know that we are getting help and doing better because of this program."

A total of thirty-four secondary students who participated in the program were interviewed, with 342 comments recorded.

Secondary students felt that academic support was the primary service, followed by personal support, developing personal and social skills, and mentoring. Secondary students felt strongly that the major benefits of participating in the program were, in rank order, academic success, having role models, improving their decision-making and problem-solving skills, and that college was a reality for them. One student shared the following:

> When I was first told that I could go to college, I wondered who was going to pay for it. Was I smart enough? And it would be so many years before I even graduate. And now, as a senior, it has all come together. But it would never have happened without my mentor in this program. For all these years, she has been with me, helping me with my schoolwork, working with my teach-

ers, and even coming to my home to work with my parents. (Female high school student)

Another student explained the importance of having positive role models in their program:

> I really like my teachers—well, most of them. But they have so many students to deal with that most of the time, they can't really help all of us. But Richard [pseudonym, NDMVA member] has been with me every day after school. He has helped me with my homework and studies, but more than that, he has showed me how to make good decisions—and then lets me try it out. I also watch how he works with other students and he acts the same way with them. Richard is a graduate of our school, went on to college, and then came back to our neighborhood to help us! (Male middle school student)

A total of twenty-three NDMVA members and teachers from participating schools were interviewed, with a total of 259 comments recorded.

An NDMVA member who works with high school students offered the following about how making a "connection" with each of the students is critical to their success:

> You can see it in their eyes . . . that once they feel connected, they really want to become great. And for some of these students, this extra help—from homework, writing papers, resolving issues—this is their first time that they have an adult outside of the home that they can trust. And remember, most of our students come to us from very large middle schools and high schools, where unfortunately it is easy to get lost. So, we provide that individual connection.

The 2015 Evaluation

The 2015 evaluation was designed to examine the impact of the services provided by NDMVA in terms of student attitudes and levels of engagement. The evaluation took place in Chicago, one of the largest, most diverse, and representative of the entire NDMVA network.

In Chicago, NDMVA supports four unique educational settings:

- The KIPP Chicago Charter Schools is part of a national network of free, open-enrollment, college preparatory public schools, serving approximately one thousand students in grades K–3 and 5–8 within four schools.
- The Marillac House and Social Center is committed to strengthening and empowering those most in need to reach their potential. To

fulfill this mission, the Marillac House offers programs and services to children, teens, families, and seniors, including an after-school program that helps students with homework, mentoring, and other small-group activities.
- The San Miguel network has campuses in two areas of Chicago, and its mission is to transform lives and neighborhoods. NDMVA members serve in classrooms as teaching assistants and provide academic and social support for high school students.
- LEARN Charter School is a network of public, college preparatory elementary schools serving almost two thousand underserved students in grades PreK–8 across five campuses. NDMVA partners serve at EXCEL Middle School, Midtown Elementary-Middle School, and True North K–8 School.[2] NDMVA members serve as teaching assistants in the classroom, run small-group learning sessions within the classrooms, and provide after-school support. (NDMVA-Chicago, n.d.)

As shown in table 3, the enrollment in these schools range from two hundred to almost five hundred students, and each has very high levels of students living in poverty, as measured by the participation rates in the federally funded Free and Reduced Lunch (FRL) program.

Table 3. 2015 Evaluation Student Survey Participants by School—Fall and Spring, by Groups (%)

School	Fall			Spring		
	Comparison	Treatment	Total	Comparison	Treatment	Total
EMS	53	41	94	41	35	76
	(56.4%)	(43.6%)	(100.0%)	(53.9%)	(46.1%)	(100.0%)
MEMS	120	107	227	136	87	223
	(53.8%)	(47.2%)	(100.0%)	(61.0%)	(39.0%)	(100.0%)
TNK8	6	6	12	6	6	12
	(50.0%)	(50.0%)	(100.0%)	(50.0%)	(50.0%)	(100.0%)
All Schools	179	154	333	183	128	311
	(53.8%)	(46.2%)	(100.0%)	(58.8%)	(41.2%)	(100.0%)

Survey Instrument

A survey was administered early in the fall of 2014 (pre) and again in late spring of 2015 (post), with both a treatment group of students and control group of students participating. In addition, randomly selected students from the treatment groups were interviewed as part of the process, following the post-survey.

The survey instrument used was The Engagement versus Disaffection with Learning Scale (Skinner, Kindermann, and Furrer, 2009). This instrument was designed to assess student motivation, including the construct of engagement versus disengagement in terms of the impact that such motivation can have on student learning, success, and achievement. This theory suggests student engagement in the learning process is enhanced when the social setting supports students' basic needs, both in a behavioral as well as emotional manner.

The instrument contains twenty-four items, divided into four subscales:

- Behavioral engagement (five items): tries, pays attention, and is persistent
- Emotional engagement (five items): motivated, taps emotions, and enjoys learning
- Behavioral disaffection (five items): lack of effort, withdraws, and pretends to pay attention
- Emotional disaffection (nine items): feeling discouraged, dislikes learning, feels frustrated during the learning process

For each item, the response scale range was 1 (not at all true), 2 (not very true), 3 (sort of true), and 4 (very true). Thus, the higher the ratings for behavioral engagement and emotional engagement, the more positively the student is motivated in school. Conversely, the higher the ratings for behavioral disaffection and emotional disaffection, the less motivated the student feels about school.

Focus Groups and Interviews

In addition to the surveys, a number of students receiving services from AmeriCorps were interviewed by the evaluator as part of the qualitative portion of the evaluation. Students were interviewed in small focus groups at the schools they attended. Student comments were transcribed and then were categorized into general trends of how the students perceived the support they were receiving. A total of twenty-one students were interviewed, with 109 comments being categorized into services, frequency of services, and benefits of services.

Quantitative Results

Evidence of success would be determined by comparing the statistical results of the fall and spring surveys in terms of changes that occurred over time within the treatment group as well as comparing changes in students' attitudes between the treatment groups and the control groups.

More than three hundred students from the three schools took both the fall and spring survey. There was a decrease in the number of students taking the survey in the spring as compared to the fall, with the treatment group decreasing from 154 to 128. One of the reasons for this decrease is that some students have become successful in school and are no longer in need of the extra support. Overall, the percentage of students in the treatment group as compared to the comparison group from fall to spring did not change significantly.

To examine the differences in student perceptions between the fall and spring surveys, mean scores and standard deviations were computed according to each of the subscales and groupings of students (control and treatment). As shown in table 4, the treatment group's difference in the mean ratings between the fall and spring was more positive in each of the four subscales.

Table 4. 2015 Evaluation: All Schools Fall/Spring Survey Differences by Treatment Group for Each Subscale

Subscale	Fall Mean (SD)	Spring Mean (SD)	t	Sig.
Behavioral Engagement	2.96 (.57)	3.25 (.63)	9.28	.001*
Emotional Engagement	2.39 (.58)	2.96 (.71)	11.61	<.001*
Behavioral Disaffection	2.28 (.54)	1.88 (.60)	7.69	.002*
Emotional Disaffection	2.42 (.57)	2.12 (.70)	7.64	.003*

To determine if such differences in the mean ratings between fall and spring were statistically significant or not, two statistical tests were applied: first, a comparison of the change in means for the control group alone, and then with the treatment group alone. For each group, a paired-sample *t*-test was used to determine if changes between the fall and spring surveys were significant. The comparison group's changes were all positive, but the changes were not statistically significant. The statistical test for the treatment group found that for each of the four subscales, the difference between the fall and spring survey were found to be positive *and* statistically significant.

Qualitative Results

The following are sample comments from students receiving NDMVA services, particularly in how the members played a role in their growth and learning.

Without the help of Miss ___ [NDMVA member], I would not be passing on to the next grade. She understood me, helped me with my reading and some math, and helped me deal with some of my problems I had with my teacher and other students. (Fifth-grade male student)

I was pulled out of my class every day. In the beginning, I didn't want to go, but then I began to like it. Miss ___ [NDMVA member] gave me lots of help that many of my friends in other classes were not able to get. I didn't like school, but I like it better now. My grades are better, and I am getting along better with others. (Fifth-grade female student)

We really trust Miss ___ [NDMVA member]. We have been with her for the whole year and she really believes in us—not all our teachers do. We all think school is a very good place to be, and we want to be good students. (Sixth-grade female student and two sixth-grade male students)

I was not doing well in school, but Miss ___ [NDMVA member] made reading and math fun for me. I like school much better now, and I really want to do well. My reading is getting better, and math is too . . . but I like reading with Miss ___ [NDMVA member] the most. (Sixth-grade female student)

The 2018 Evaluation

For the 2018 evaluation, three sites were selected as a representative sample of the entire NDMVA program: Baltimore, Greater Boston, and New Orleans. The primary evaluation questions considered were:

1. Do students who receive in-school academic support services through services provided by NDMVA improve their levels of school engagement over the course of a school year?
2. To what extent do the demographics of students who receive academic support services from NDMVA impact the level of changes of school engagement over the course of a year?
3. Do students who receive in-school academic support services provided by NDMVA improve their levels of school engagement more than students who do not receive such services over the course of a school year?

Evaluation Locations

Baltimore. Overall, NDMVA Baltimore has twelve sites and eighteen members who serve almost four hundred students. The sites include public charter schools, private schools, and Catholic schools. Members assist students by providing one-on-one and small-group tutoring in regular classes and outside of class.

Greater Boston. The Greater Boston Education Award Partners of Notre Dame Mission Volunteers–AmeriCorps is a network that includes eleven schools and educational programing sites in the Greater Boston area that specifically work to educate economically disadvantaged students in a holistic learning community. Most of the schools/sites have roots within the Catholic and/or Nativity network schools. They are private, tuition-free schools with small classroom sizes, offering extended day programming, free meals throughout the day (many including dinner most evenings as well), evening study sessions, and other support services.

New Orleans. Notre Dame–AmeriCorps New Orleans works to provide valuable support in schools, educational programs, and nonprofits. The mission is to provide direct service support to local organizations in the New Orleans area who serve underprivileged communities. Most members help with school literacy programs by serving alongside the head librarian and implementing small reading groups. Through this support, AmeriCorps members have increased library circulation by over 1,000 percent at some schools and have really fostered a strong culture of reading over the years of service.

Survey Instrument

The Student Engagement Instrument (Appleton et al., 2006) was used as the primary quantitative measurement for collecting data for the 2018 evaluation. The construct of this instrument suggests that student engagement is a key factor in support of student learning and achievement (Connell, 1990; Connell and Wellborn, 1991). The instrument contains two general scales that measure both affective engagement (level of interest in learning) and cognitive engagement (beliefs and ideas about learning). For the affective engagement (AE) scale, there are three subscales:

- Teacher-student relationships (TSR; nine items)
- Peer support for learning (PSL; six items)
- Family support for learning (FSL; four items)

For the cognitive engagement scale (CE), there are also three subscales:

- Control and relevance to school work (CRSW; nine items)
- Future goals and aspirations (FGA; five items)
- Intrinsic motivation (IM; two items)

The scoring of the instrument for each of the thirty-five items is a four-point scale that ranges from strongly disagree (1) to strongly agree (4).

70 ~ Chapter Four

In addition, demographic information was collected from each participant who completed both surveys, including gender, treatment or control group, ethnicity, grade, and location.

Focus Groups and Interviews

The purpose of the qualitative portion of the evaluation was for the evaluator to develop a better understanding of the meanings constructed by students who participate in the NDMVA program in the Baltimore, Greater Boston, and New Orleans sites. Unlike the quantitative portion, this part of the evaluation sought to interpret, translate, and assess student experiences, particularly as they relate to the unique features of the NDMVA program. A total of forty-one students from the three cities participated in the focus group discussions, each lasting about thirty minutes.

Quantitative Results

During the fall of 2017, a total of 382 students across three sites took the survey, and then in the spring of 2018, 362 students took the survey. Of this, 341 students were able to be matched between the fall and spring through the use of their unique identification numbers. From the total of 341 matched surveys, 302 students from the treatment group were identified as receiving services, and 39 students were identified from the control group.

In addition, the matched surveys came from the following sites: Baltimore: 45 (13.2%), Greater Boston: 220 (64.5%), and New Orleans: 76 (22.3%).

Data Analysis-Evaluation Question 1. To answer the first evaluation question, the evaluator performed a paired samples t-test, which was used to analyze the spring survey results with the fall results of the treatment group only.

A total of 302 students in the treatment group were identified as taking both the pre- and the post-survey. As shown in table 5, the students in the treatment group had statistically significant increases in each of the six subscales. There was a statistically significant increase for the treatment students in each of the six subscales.

Data Analysis-Evaluation Question 2. The second analysis was conducted to determine if the demographics (gender, ethnicity, grade, and location) of the students in the treatment group influenced the difference between results found in the pre- and post-surveys. While there were differences found between the pre- and post-survey among the various demographic groups within the treatment sample, none were found to be statistically significant.

Data Analysis-Evaluation Question 3. A third analysis was conducted to determine whether there were differences found between the pre- and post-

Table 5. Paired Sample T-Test for Treatment Group by Subscales (N=302)

Subscale	Pre-Survey Mean (SD)	Post-Survey Mean (SD)	Mean Diff. (SD)	p*
Teacher-Student Relationship (TSR)	2.97 (.39)	3.13 (.36)	.14 (.55)	0.00
Peer Support for Learning (PSL)	3.29 (.41)	3.44 (.35)	.15 (.55)	0.00
Family Support for Learning (FSL)	3.29 (.46)	3.42 (.38)	.13 (.58)	0.00
Control and Relevance to School Work (CRSW)	2.87 (.41)	3.02 (.35)	.15 (.38)	0.00
Future Goals and Aspirations (FGA)	2.97 (.41)	3.12 (.34)	.15 (.49)	0.00
Intrinsic Motivation (IM)	3.34 (.60)	3.49 (.54)	.15 (.67)	0.00

surveys in the relationship between the treatment group and control group. Since there were only thirty-nine students in the control group who were identified as taking both the pre- and post-survey, the evaluator randomly selected thirty-nine students from the treatment groups to compare the results.

The treatment group saw an increase between the pre- and post-survey, which was higher in five of the six subscales (TSR, PSL, FSL, FGA, and IM). The only subscale in which the control group had a higher increase was CRSW. It should also be noted that in five of the six subscales, the mean difference among the control group actually decreased, with the only increase being the CRSW subscale.

To determine if the differences in the increase between the pre- and post-survey regarding the treatment and control group was statistically significant, an independent sample *t*-test was conducted. As shown in table 6, the differ-

Table 6. 2018 Evaluation: Independent Sample T-Test of Difference Between Pre- and Post-Surveys by Treatment and Control Groups

Subscales	t	df	Mean Diff.	p
Teacher-Student Relationships (TSR)	2.42	76	.28	.018*
Peer Support for Learning (PSL)	1.57	76	.22	.119
Family Support for Learning (FSL)	2.23	76	.26	.049*
Control and Relevance to School Work (CRSW)	–.305	76	–.02	.761
Future Goals and Aspirations (FGA)	3.24	76	.33	.002
Intrinsic Motivation (IM)	2.23	76	.20	.044

*statistically significant at .05 or less

ences in the mean between the pre-survey and the post-survey were found to be statistically significant in four of the six subscales: TSR, FSL, FGA, and IM. Statistical significance was not found in the PSL and CRSW subscales.

Qualitative Results

A sample of students receiving services from NDMVA were interviewed by the evaluator. Students were in groups of three to five, and each of the interviews lasted about thirty minutes. At total of forty-one students from the three cities were interviewed.

Below is a sample of quotes from students who were part of the interviews and focus groups, which describe the positive nature of their experiences.

> I feel much better about school and friends now than I have before. Mr. _____ [NDMVA member] always checked up on me, helped me with my reading, and always had good things to say to me. (Fifth-grade male student)

> Ms. _____ [NDMVA member] would never let me fail. Math has always been a hard subject for me and my two friends here, but she would work with us before school, during school, and after school. And I know she had other students to work with, but she would always find me (and us) and help us with our work. (Sixth-grade female student)

> In the beginning of the year, we all thought that we were getting help from Ms. ___ and Ms. ___ [NDMVA members] because we weren't very smart. But the more we met with them, the better it felt to go to school and the better we did in school. Both of them are leaving at the end of the year, and we hope that we get helpers like this next year. (Three seventh-grade female students)

Discussion and Conclusion

Notre Dame Mission Volunteers–AmeriCorps is an exemplary initiative that is making a significant impact on the lives of the students enrolled in its various programs. Thousands of students across the nation are being supported, mentored, and motivated to levels of achievement and personal development that may not have occurred otherwise.

Analysis of the student achievement data provides very strong evidence of the impact the programs are having on students' academic success and their attitudes, based on the number of statistical analyses completed in the three evaluations.

Interviews of students and NDMVA members substantiated the findings from the three evaluations. Overwhelmingly, students felt very appreciative of the services they received in academics, emotionally, and socially. Of particular note, students felt a considerable and positive attachment to the NDMVA members who supported and mentored them in the program. The NDMVA members also provided very positive perceptions of the program and the impact they have on the students, with many comments about the critical nature of being role models, being passionate about what NDMVA members do, and their devotion to the program and students.

From the perspective of this author, there are two major reasons for the success of this program. First, there is a total and comprehensive commitment by NDMVA in support of its mission, which then is transferred into effective planning, actions, and positive results. Also, there is a strong commitment by the NDMVA administration to ensure that all directors and members receive training and support on a regular basis.

Second, positive relationships are built between the members and the students they serve, viewing each student through the asset model (by seeing what is good in the child, family, and/or community) rather than the traditional deficit model (which views the child in terms of what he or she does not have or is not doing, based on his or her environment).

NDMVA members live and serve alongside the communities where they are providing educational support, allowing the community to view the volunteers as contributing members of society who, first and foremost, serve others.

In conclusion, the analysis of both quantitative and qualitative data provided very strong evidence that the NDMVA program is a robust network of support for at-risk and marginalized students. In many cases, student attitudes throughout the year improved significantly. Both students and school staff provided many positive examples of the program's success. There was a positive correlation between student attitudes and student achievement in the overall NDMVA program. It is clear that Notre Dame Mission Volunteers–AmeriCorps is not just another government program supporting marginalized students. It is a shining example of what effective collaboration among government institutions, social justice organizations, and local schools can look like in support of young people who, through no fault of their own, have been relegated to the margins of society.

A teacher who has worked directly with NDMVA members for several years shared the following:

> If there was no program, then what would these kids do? Where would the support come from? As a teacher I can't do it alone, but this support does make a difference, and these kids need us and want what we do. And, these kids, for the most part, are society's most vulnerable students. With class sizes so large,

my students do not get the help and support they need. And, from the bigger picture, our country will be worse off because the socioeconomic-educational gap will only get wider. (Male middle school teacher)

Finally, the NDMVA program is a lesson on leadership—not so much the traditional, hierarchical type but more of an intersection of leadership for social justice, servant leadership, and volunteerism driven by a social and ethical mission to ensure all students have opportunities for equality and equity in terms of social, economic, and political constructs. And, while students are the recipients of the efforts of NDMVA to ensure such opportunities, it should not be lost on anyone that, in fact, the entire network of NDMVA is providing a model of how such programs can be both relevant and successful in a world where many students are often left behind.

Notes

1. The terms *volunteer* and *member* will be used interchangeably throughout this chapter.
2. The names of the three schools are pseudonyms.

References

Allen, L. (2006). The moral life of schools revisited: Preparing educational leaders to build a new social order for social justice and democratic community. *International Journal of Urban Educational Leadership, 1*, 1–13.

Appleton, J., Christenson, S., and Furlong, M. (2008). Student engagement with school: Critical conceptual and methodological issues of construct. *Psychology in the Schools, 45*, 369–86.

Appleton, J., Christenson, S. L., Kim, D., and Reschly, A. L. (2006). Measuring cognitive and psychological engagement: Validation of the student engagement instrument. *Journal of School Psychology, 44*, 427–45.

Center for Disease Control and Prevention. (2018). *Program operations and guidelines*. Available at https://www.cdc.gov/eval/.

Connell, J. P. (1990). Context, self and action: a motivational analysis of self-system processes across the life-span. In D. Cicchetti (Ed.), *The self in transition: Infancy to childhood*. Chicago, IL: University of Chicago.

Connell, J. P., and Wellborn, J. G. (1991). Competence, autonomy, and relatedness: A motivational analysis of self-system process. In M. R. Gunnar and L. A. Sroufe (Eds.), *Self-processes and development: Minnesota Symposium on Child Psychology* (Volume 23). Chicago, IL: University of Chicago.

Corporation for National and Community Service. (n.d.). *AmeriCorps and Senior Corps*. Retrieved from https://www.nationalservice.gov/programs/americorps.

Evans, A. (2007). Horton, Highlander, and leadership education: Lessons for preparing educational leaders for social justice. *Journal of School Leadership, 17,* 250–75.

Greenleaf, R. (1970). *The servant as leader.* Westfield, IN: Greenleaf Center for Servant Leadership.

Haski-Leventhal, D. (2009). Altruism and volunteerism: The perceptions of altruism in four disciplines and their impact on the study of volunteerism. *Journal for the Theory of Social Behaviors, 39*(3), 271–99.

Jean-Marie, G. (2008). Leadership for social justice: An agenda for 21st century schools. *The Educational Forum, 72,* 340–54.

Libbey, H. (2004). Measuring student relationships to school: Attachment, bonding, connectedness, and engagement. *Journal of School Health, 74,* 274–83.

Maxfield, M., and Babbie, E. (2008). *Basics of research methods for criminal justice and criminology* (second edition). Belmont, CA: Wadsworth.

Northouse, P. (2016). *Leadership: Theory and practice* (seventh edition). Thousand Oaks, CA: Sage.

Notre Dame Mission Volunteer AmeriCorps. (2017). *Mission Statement.* Retrieved from http://www.ndmva.org/learn.

Penner, L. (2002). Dispositional and organizational influences on volunteerism: An interactive perspective. *Journal of Social Issues, 58*(3), 447–67.

Rossi, P., Freeman, H., and Lipsey, M. (2003). *Evaluation—a systematic approach* (seventh edition). Thousand Oaks, CA: Sage.

Skinner, E., Kindermann, T., and Furrer, C. (2009). A motivational perspective on engagement and disaffection: Conceptualization and assessment of children's behavioral and emotional participation in academic activities in the classroom. *Educational and Psychological Measurement, 69,* 493–525.

About the Authors

Susan Toft Everson is an associate professor of educational leadership at Saint Louis University. As senior director at McREL, a federally funded educational R&D laboratory, she has led improvement, educational change, and leadership initiatives. She has co-edited two books on school reform, published numerous articles, and has consulted in the United States and Europe.

Tanyathorn Hauwadhanasuk is a PhD candidate in special education, research minor, at Saint Louis University (SLU). Her research and publications focus on special education, inclusive education, and autism. Tanya is the author of a number of chapters in books and scholarly articles. She serves as a secretary of SLU Chapter Sigma Xi, Scientific Honor Society.

Mustafa Karnas is a PhD candidate in special education at Saint Louis University. His research interests include autism, educational leadership, and policy analysis. He is a co-author of a published article and has presented at numerous national and international conferences.

Adam E. Nir is a professor of educational administration policy and leadership and the Abraham Shiffman Chair in Secondary Education at the Hebrew University of Jerusalem, Israel. He is the former chair of the Department of Education at the Hebrew University and the former president of the International Society for Educational Planning. His research interests include school autonomy, school-based management, educational planning, leadership, and human resource management in public education.

Calvin G. Roso is a professor of educational leadership at Azusa Pacific University, located in Los Angeles County, California. His research interests include religion and academics, effective teaching, and service learning. He has also served in teacher professional development and K–12 accreditation in the United States and multiple other countries since 1995.

Shenggang Yu is a professor and dean of the School of Education, Beihua University, China. Dr. Yu's research focuses on teacher education and leadership in higher education. His published work deals with design and assessment of university academic management and curriculum design for pre-teacher teaching skills.

Min Zhuang is a PhD student in the Educational Foundation Program at Saint Louis University. Her research interests include inclusive education and LGBTQ issues in education. Zhuang has over three years of experience in teaching Mandarin at Saint Louis University.

About the Editor

Peter R. Litchka is a professor of educational leadership at Loyola University Maryland, where he has been since 2006. Prior to coming to Loyola, Peter was in public education for thirty-three years, including being a classroom teacher, a school and district administrator, and twice a superintendent of schools in New York state. He is author/co-author of three books in educational leadership and numerous scholarly articles and has presented in the United States as well as in Canada, Cyprus, Israel, Poland, and Turkey. Peter received his bachelor's degree from the State University of New York at Geneseo, his master's degree from Johns Hopkins University, and his doctorate from Seton Hall University. He is currently president of the International Society for Educational Planning.

Other books by Peter Litchka:

The Dark Side of Educational Leadership—Superintendents and the Professional Victim Syndrome (with Walter Polka, 2008)

Living on the Horns of Dilemmas—Superintendents, Politics and Decision-Making (with Walter Polka and Frank Calzi, 2014)

Exemplary Leadership Practices—Learning from the Past to Enhance Future School Leadership (2016)

www.ingramcontent.com/pod-product-compliance
Lightning Source LLC
Chambersburg PA
CBHW021215240426
43672CB00026B/320